Disaster Mangement

Disaster Mangement

Ramakant Gaur

AUTHORSPRESS
Publishers of Creative & Scholarly Books

Worldwide Circulation through Authorspress Global Network
First Published in 2008
by
Authorspress
Q-2A Hauz Khas Enclave, New Delhi-110 016 (India)
Phone: (0) 9818049852
E-mail: authorspressgroup@gmail.com
Website: www.authorspressbooks.com

Disaster Mangement

ISBN 81-89012-46-0

Printed in India at Kensington Press

Preface

Disasters, whether man-made or natural, have always been an inevitable component of human life. Wars, fires, earthquakes, volcanic disruptions, floods, cylones, tsunamis, etc., have managed to wreak immense havoc on humanity, bringing in loss of both life and property. In recent history the 2004 South Asian Tsunami was a disaster whose memory is still imprinted on the minds of the millions who were seriously affected, whether emotionally, financially or physically. Disaster management, herein, serves as an important field, which looks into the methodology and practice of dealing with and avoiding risks.

This book, meant to serve the needs of those pursing their Masters' in Education, books into the discipline of disaster management. Written as an introductory manual, the book takes a multidimensional approach to the discussion of the subject, which involves preparing, supporting and rebuilding society when natural or human made disasters occur. Involving the process of mitigation, preparedness, response and recovery, disaster management is multilayerd, bringing within its purview a whole range of conditions and task. The book engages in a full-fledged discussion of the practices, processes, techniques, equipment and managerial strategies involved, both in pre- as as well as post-disaster condition. Delving into specific disaster scenarios, the book manages to convey to the readers essential information on what to do in case of unprecedented disasters as well as informing them academically on the issue. It also takes a book at current trends in the field, making a survey of future developments.

It is hoped that the comprehensive and insightful content of the book prove satisfactory to the readers.

Ramakant Gaur

Contents

CHAPTER 1

Introduction to Disaster Management

1.1. Introduction

A disaster is a serious disruption of the functioning of a society, causing widespread human, material, or environmental losses, which exceed the ability of affected society to copy using only its own resources. Disasters are often classified according to their speed of onset (sudden or slow), or according to their cause (natural or man-made).

1.1.1. Natural Phenomena

These are extreme climatological, hydrological, or geological, processes that do not pose any threat to persons or property. A massive earthquake in an unpopulated area, for example, is a natural phenomena, not a hazard.

1.1.2. Emergency

A disaster might be regarded as a particular type (or sub-set) of an emergency. "Disaster" suggests an intense time period and level of urgency. Whereas a disaster is bound by a specific period in which lives and essential property are immediately at risk, an emergency can encompass a more general period in which there is a clear and marked deterioration in the coping abilities of a group or community, or coping abilities are only sustained by unusual initiatives by the group or community or by external intervention.

1.1.3. Disaster Problem

Disasters and emergencies are fundamental reflections of normal life. They are consequences of the ways societies structure themselves, economically and socially; the ways that societies and states interact; and the ways that relationships between the decision makers are sustained. Hence a flood or an earthquake is not a disaster in and of itself.

The magnitude of each disaster, measured in deaths, damage, or costs for a given developing country increases with the increased marginalisation of the population. This is caused by a high birthrate, problems of land tenure and economic opportunity, and the lack or misallocation of resources to meet the basic human needs of an expanding population. As the population increases, the best land in both rural and urban areas is taken up, and those seeking land for farming or housing are forced to accept inadequate land. These offer less productivity and a smaller measure of physical or economic safety.

1.2. Disaster Management

1.2.1. Poverty

The most important single influence on the impact of a disaster is poverty. All other factors could be lessened if the affected population were not also limited by poverty. Virtually all disaster studies show that the wealthiest of the population either survive the disaster unaffected or are able to recover quickly. Across the broad spectrum of disasters, poverty generally makes people vulnerable to the impact of hazards. Poverty explains why people in urban areas are forced to live on hills that are prone to landslides, or why people settle near volcanoes or rivers that invariably flood their banks. Poverty explains why droughts claim poor peasant farmers as victims an rarely the wealthy, and why famines more other than not are the result of a lack of purchasing power to buy food rather than an absence of food. Increasingly, poverty also explains why many people are forced to move from their homes to other parts of their countries or even across borders to survive. Such crisis-induced migration poses considerable challenges both in terms of immediate assistance to the displaced and of longer-term development.

1.2.2. Population Growth

There is an obvious connection between the increase in losses from a disaster and the increase in population. If there are more people and structures where a disaster strikes, then it is likely there will be more of an impact. The growth of population has been so spectacular that it is inevitable that more people will be affected by disaster because more will be forced to live and work in unsafe areas. Increasing numbers of people will be competing for a limited amount of resources (such as, employment opportunities, and land), which can lead to conflict. This conflict may result in crisis-induced migration. Such growth occurs predominantly in developing countries, resulting in various contributors to disasters.

1.2.3. Rapid Urbanisation

Rapid population growth and migration are related to the major phenomenon of rapid urbanisation. This process is also accelerated in developing countries. It is characterised by the rural poor or civilians in an area of conflict moving to metropolitan areas in search of economic opportunities and security. These massive numbers of urban poor increasingly find fewer options for availability of safe and desirable places to build their houses. Here again, competition for scare resources, an inevitable consequence of rapid urbanisation, can lead to human-made disasters. Many landslides or flooding disasters are closely linked to rapid and unchecked urbanisation, which forces low-income families to settle on the slopes of steep hillsides or ravines, or along the banks of flood-prone rivers. Many earthquake victims in urban areas have been impoverished families whose sites have failed rather than their houses, usually through landslides onto the house or out from under it.

1.2.4. Transitions in Cultural Practices

Many of the inevitable changes that occur in all societies lead to an increase in the societies' vulnerability to disasters. Obviously, all societies are constantly changing and in a continual state of transition. These transitions are often extremely disruptive and uneven, leaving gaps in social coping mechanisms and technology. These transitions include nomadic populations that become sedentary rural people who move to urban areas, and both rural and urban people who move from one economic level to another. More broadly, these examples are typical of a shift from non-industrialised to industrialising societies.

One example of the impact of these transitions is the introduction of new construction materials and building designs in a society that is accustomed to traditional materials and designs. This often results in new materials being used incorrectly. In disaster prone areas, inadequate new construction techniques may lead to houses that cannot withstand earthquakes or wind Storms. Compounding this problem is the new community where the disaster survivors find themselves may not have a social support system or network to assist in the relief and recovery from the disaster. The traditional coping mechanisms may not exist in the new setting and the population becomes increasingly dependent on outside interveners to help in this process. Conflicting as well as transitional cultural practices can also lead to civil conflict, for example, as a result of communal violence triggered by religious differences.

1.2.5. Environmental Degradation

Many disasters are either caused or exacerbated by environmental degradation. Deforestation leads to rapid rain run off, which contributes to flooding. The destruction of mangrove swamps decreases a coastline's ability to resist tropical winds and storm surges. The creation of drought conditions-and the relative severity and length of time the drought lasts-is mainly a natural phenomenon. Drought conditions may be exacerbated by: poor cropping patterns, overgrasing, the stripping of topsoil, poor conservation techniques, depletion of both the surface and subsurface water supply, and, to an extent, unchecked urbanisation.

1.2.6. Lack of Awareness and Information

Disasters can also happen because people vulnerable to them simply didn't know how to get out of harm's way or to take protective measures. This ignorance may not necessarily be a function of poverty, but a lack of awareness of what measures can be taken to build safe structures on safe locations. Perhaps some people did not know about safe evacuation routes and procedures. Other populations may not know where to turn for assistance in times of acute distress. Nevertheless, this point should not be taken as a justification for ignoring the coping mechanisms of the majority of people affected by disasters. In most disaster-prone societies, there is a wealth of understanding about disaster threats and responses. This understanding should be incorporated into any efforts to provide external assistance.

1.2.7. War and Civil Strife

War and civil strife often result in displaced people, a target population of this training programme. The causal factors of war and civil strife include competition for scarce resources, religious or ethnic intolerance, and ideological differences. Many of these are also byproducts of the preceding six causal factors of disasters.

Human-made disasters are disasters or emergency situations where the principal, direct cause(s) are identifiable human actions, deliberate or otherwise. Apart from "technological" and "ecological" disasters, this mainly involves situations in which civilian populations suffer casualties, losses of property, basic services and means of livelihood as a result of war or civil strife. Human-made disasters/emergencies can be of the rapid or slow onset types, and in the case of internal conflict, can lead to "complex emergencies" as well.

1.2.8. Impact on Investment Climate

Disasters, especially when they have occurred repeatedly within a short period of time, have a negative impact on the incentive for further investment. Investors need a climate of stability and certainty to be encouraged to risk their money. The disaster further clouds the investment picture when it has caused loss of employment, thereby depressing market demand, and resulting in a stagnation, which limits overall growth.

1.2.9. Impact on Non-formal Sector

Disasters have special negative impacts on the non-formal sector where approximate costs of disasters are often underestimated. Disasters depress the non-formal economy through the direct costs of lost equipment and housing. The indirect costs of disasters include lost employment, and lost income. Sometimes the importation of relief items creates disincentives to producers.

1.2.10. Political Destabilisation

The stress to a country caused by a disaster often results in the destabilisation of the government. This may occur for several reasons. For example, the government may have mismanaged the disaster relief and recovery, leading to discontent on the part of affected communities. Or the survivors may have had unmet expectation which, for whatever reason, translate into some form of protest. The government could also become the scapegoat for problems beyond its control, again leading to its possible downfall. In fact, it is very common for a government to collapse or be overthrown within two or three years of a major disaster.

1.2.11. Side Effects of Development

The side effects of well-meaning development efforts sometimes have disastrous consequences. Development projects implemented without taking into account existing environmental hazards may increase vulnerability to natural disasters. Low-income people may then have to seek housing in areas previously avoided, on hillsides or in floodplains. The costs of relief assistance after a landslide or flood can easily outweigh the benefits to the economy of more jobs. Similarly, development projects may lead to negative political consequences that increase the vulnerability to civil conflict. Some types of development projects commence without fully assessing their impact on the environment. This can occur even in programmes resulting from a disaster, such as reconstruction projects that increase demand for wood to fortify houses. The resulting deforestation can then bring increased vulnerability to mudslides and possibly long-term environmental changes. Development projects may even consciously force a choice between reducing disaster vulnerability and economic vulnerability. A project's design may require a trade-off between the two and force a decision between the lesser of two evils.

Despite an increasing disaster awareness in the international community, and the recognition of the importance of developing coherent plans for relief activities, it often takes the actual or imminent occurrence of a large-scale destructive event to stimulate individual governments to think about a developmental approach. Thus, a disaster can serve as a catalyst for introducing mitigation activities. Few development workers realise the opportunities that disasters can provide in the development field. Disasters often create a political and economic atmosphere wherein extensive changes can be made more rapidly than under normal circumstances. For example, in the aftermath of a disaster, there may be major opportunities to execute land reform programmes, to improve the overall housing stock, to create new jobs and job skills, and to expand and modernise the economic base of the community-opportunities that would not otherwise be possible. The collective will to take action is an advantage that should not be wasted.

Disasters can also highlight high-risk areas where action must be taken before another disaster strikes. The realisation of vulnerability can motivate policy-makers and the public to participate in mitigation activities. Disasters may also serve to highlight the fact that the country is seriously under-developed. They can thus bring in funding and the attention of donor communities to apply to long-term development needs.

1.3. Natural Hazards

Disasters and emergencies resulting from natural and human-made hazards have been developed in general terms. However, each hazard has its own characteristics. Many occur infrequently or impact a very small population. Other hazards, such as severe snowstorms, often occur in areas that are prepared to deal with them and seldom become disasters. However, from the perspective of a disaster victim it is not particularly useful to distinguish between minor and major disasters. Some disasters are now of limited interest to the international community. These include avalanches, fog, frost, hail, lightning, snowstorms, and tornadoes. The international interest is less for these hazards because their impacts affect relatively few people and the countries in which they normally occur have sufficient resources and systems in place to respond without external assistance.

1.3.1. Socio/political Forces

Increasingly throughout many parts of the world one type of hazard can trigger a disaster which in turn triggers another hazard and subsequent disaster. For example, a drought may lead to a famine which in turn leads to a civil conflict that results in the mass displacement of people. A flood may force people to seek refuge across an international border where conflicts ensue between refugees and local communities. Such compound hazards and disasters need not happen sequentially; they can also occur simultaneously. Thus, people caught between contending forces in a civil war find that in the midst of a major drought they have no means either to grow food or to receive outside assistance.

In a growing number of countries, complex disasters are also becoming more evident. Essentially a complex disaster is a form of a human-made emergency in which the cause of the emergency as well as the assistance to the afflicted are bound by intense levels of political considerations. The single most prevalent political condition of a complex emergency is civil conflict, resulting in a collapse of political authority in all or part of a country.

The disaster becomes "complex" because either the collapse or diffusion of political control makes assistance highly problematic. Solutions ultimately depend upon agreements with all parties involved in the conflict to permit assistance to be provided to recognise civilian non-combatants. These solutions may be agreements that are seen essentially as compromising fundamental aspects of sovereignty for what have been labelled as "new mechanisms of humanitarian assistance."

1.4. Components of Disaster Preparedness

There are nine major components involved in disaster preparedness, which provide a framework upon which a national disaster preparedness strategy can be developed.

1.4.1. Assessing Vulnerability

Fundamental to all aspects of disaster management is information. It is a point that may appear obvious, but it is frequently overlooked. The disaster manager may know that a particular geographic region or community is susceptible to the impacts of sudden or slow-onset hazards. However, in reality, until a decision is made on systematic ways to compile and assess information about disaster vulnerabilities, the manager is and will be working in a void.

Developing and compiling vulnerability assessments is one way of approaching a systematic means of establishing an essential disaster management tool.

1.4.2. Planning

Throughout all the activities designed to promote disaster preparedness, the ultimate objective is to have plans in place that are agreed upon, that are implementable and for which commitment and resources are relatively assured. The plan itself will have to address other points in this framework.

1.4.3. Institutional Framework

A coordinated disaster preparedness and response system is a prerequisite to any disaster preparedness plan. Each system design will depend upon the traditions and governmental structure of the country under review. However, without ensuring that there is "horizontal coordination" at central government levels among ministries and specialised government bodies and "vertical coordination" between central and local authorities, a plan will rapidly disintegrate. This requires a structure for decision-making, inter-ministerial committees to coordinate the plan, focal points within each ministry to be responsible for the plan implementation and communication, as well as regional and community structures to implement the plan at the local level.

1.4.4. Information Systems

The preparedness plan must have an information system. For slow onset disasters this should consist of a formalised data collection process, and early warning system, and monitoring system to update the early warning information. For sudden onset disasters a similar system must be in place for prediction, warning, and evacuation communication.

1.4.5. Resource Base

The requirements to meet an emergency situation will clearly depend upon the types of hazards the plan anticipates. Such requirements should be made explicit, and should cover all aspects of disaster relief and recovery implementation. The following are the major requirements:

1.4.5.1. Warning systems

For most types of rapid onset disasters, a warning system can save many lives. By giving a vulnerable population adequate notice of an impending disaster, they can either escape the event or take precautions to reduce the dangers. However, you must assume that functioning communications systems, such as telephones and telexes, may not be available in times of a major disaster. Begin to plan a warning system around that assumption. Consider what type of communications equipment will be needed and sustainable if power lines and receiving stations are destroyed. Preparedness plans should include provisions for access to alternative communication systems among police, military and government networks.

1.4.5.2. Response mechanisms

The plan's ultimate test is the effectiveness of response to warnings and disaster impacts. At a certain stage in the warning process, various responses will have to be mobilised. The staging of responses becomes an essential factor in designing a preparedness plan.

1.4.5.3. Public education and training

The focus of a disaster preparedness plan should be to anticipate, to the extent possible, the types of requirements needed for action or responses to warnings and a disaster relief operation. The plan should also specify the most effective ways of ensuring that such requirements are met. Yet, the process will only be effective if those who are the ultimate beneficiaries know what to do in times of disasters and know what to expect.

1.4.5.4. Slow and sudden onset disasters

Preparedness activities for slow onset disasters often vary from those of sudden onset. Slow onset disasters may require more active involvement on the part of planners, especially in terms of monitoring early warning systems, for famine, war, and civil strife. The remedial response to problems indicated by the early warning is an extension of preparedness. Preparedness for sudden onset disasters includes the monitoring of the predictions and warnings of disasters that may occur within a matter of days or hours. The emergency may develop over a very brief time frame and depend on a very different set of procedures and resources than the slow onset emergency.

1.4.6. Vulnerability and Risk Assessment

1.4.6.1. Risk management

The overall task of risk management must include both an estimation of the magnitude of a particular risk and an evaluation of how important to us the risk is. The process of risk management therefore has two parts: risk assessment and risk evaluation. Risk assessment requires the quantification of the risk from data and understanding the processes involved. Risk evaluation is the judgement that a society places on the risks that face them in deciding what to do about them.

The first step in risk management is quantifying the probability of the risk. The second step is evaluating the risk, that is, passing judgement on how serious it is. The importance a community places on the risk of a disaster is likely to be influenced by the type and level of other everyday risks it faces. Even if the risk from a natural hazard is quite significant, it is unlikely to compare, for example, with the risk of child mortality in a society with minimal primary health care.

Villages in the hazardous mountain valleys of Northern Pakistan, regularly afflicted by floods, earthquakes, and landslides, do not perceive disaster mitigation to be one of their priorities. Their priorities are protection against the greater risks of disease and irrigation failures. As societies develop economically, risk reduction is likely to assume greater importance to them. Development itself can increase the likelihood of disasters, but as societies become richer more resources can be made available to invest in some degree of protection. Protection of the development process itself becomes a disaster mitigation issue.

1.4.6.2. Acceptable levels of risk

Many risks are associated with benefits. Living close to a volcano may bring the benefit of fertile soils for good agriculture. Generally, though, the exposure to natural and environmental hazards does not have any specific benefit associated with it-the exposure is a simple consequence of living or working in a particular location. This can have the effects of making such risks less acceptable than those from which some benefit is obtained. Generally the acceptable levels of risk appear to increase according to the benefits derived from being exposed to it. However, the acceptable level of risk appears to decrease over time as more people become exposed to a particular type of risk.

1.4.6.3. Assessing risk and vulnerability

The estimation of probably future losses is a matter of increasing interest to those concerned with development planning in hazard-prone regions. Fundamental to disaster preparedness and mitigation planning is an understanding of what to expect. This needs to be quantified, if only in a crude and approximate way, in terms of the degree of risk faced, the size of event that is likely, and the consequences of an event if it occurs. The calculation of risk generally needs to consider several types of loss. The most common parameter of loss, and the one most easily dealt with, is economic cost. Cost is widely used because many types of loss can be converted into economic cost. Effects, which are considered in terms of economic costs, are known as tangible losses. But there are a range of other effects resulting from disasters which are important but which cannot be converted into a monetary equivalent, and these are referred to as intangible losses. A full consideration of risk would include a complete range of effects, both tangible and intangible, and of several qualitatively different types.

1.4.7. Response of Disaster

Disaster response is the sum total of actions taken by people and institutions in the face of disaster. These actions commence with the warning of an oncoming threatening event or with the event itself if it occurs without warning. Disaster response includes the implementation of disaster preparedness plans and procedures, thus overlapping with disaster preparedness. The end of disaster response comes with the completion of response comes with the completion of disaster rehabilitation programmes. Disaster response activities are implemented by a myriad of government organisations, international and national agencies, local entities and individuals, each with their roles and responsibilities.

1.5. Disaster Assessment

Assessment is the process of determining the impact of a disaster on a society. The first priority is to establish the needs for immediate emergency measures to save and sustain the lives of survivors. The second priority is to identify the possibilities for facilitating and expediting recovery and development. Assessment is an interdisciplinary process undertaken in phases and involving on-the-spot surveys and the collation, evaluation and interpretation of information from various sources. These surveys concern both direct and indirect losses as well as the short- and long-term effects. Assessment involves determining not only what has happened and what assistance might be needed, but also defines objectives and how relevant assistance can actually be provided to the victims.

Some assessments are specifically conducted as damage assessments. They include the preparation of specific, quantified estimates of physical damage resulting from a disaster. The damage assessment may also include recommendations concerning the repair, reconstruction or replacement of structures, and equipment, as well as the restoration of economic activities.

1.5.1. Objectives of Assessment

The first objective of a post-disaster assessment is to determine when an emergency exists. Next, define the actions and resources needed to reduce immediate threats to health and safety and to pre-empt future serious problems. A frequent problem of assessment is to assume that all property losses or survival needs must be replaced or furnished from outside sources only. Instead the assessment must also identify the local response capacity, including organisational, medical, and logistical resources. The assessment must help decide how best to use existing resources for relief. It must also identify the priorities of the affected people themselves. Another problem is that people making the assessment who are not from the disaster area may have a difficult time distinguishing chronic needs from problems created by the disaster. Knowledge of base line data is essential to identify the "starting point" for post-disaster needs. If the results of the assessment are to contribute to the design of a disaster response program, then the response agency must also know the policies of the government with regard to emergency assistance. These policies will affect the estimate for the additional support required from national and international sources for relief.

1.5.2. Rehabilitation and Reconstruction

Rehabilitation and reconstruction comprise most of the disaster recovery phase. This period following the emergency phase focuses on activities that enable victims to resume normal, viable lives and means of livelihood. It also includes the restoration of infrastructure, services and the economy in a manner appropriate to long-term needs and defined development objectives. Nevertheless, after some disasters, there also may be a need for continuing humanitarian assistance for selected vulnerable groups.

Rehabilitation is the actions taken in the aftermath of a disaster to enable basic services to resume functioning, assist victims' self-help efforts to repair dwellings and community facilities, and facilitate the revival of economic activities. Rehabilitation focuses on enabling the affected populations to resume more-or-less normal patterns of life.

Reconstruction is the permanent construction or replacement of severely damaged physical structures, the full restoration of all services and local infrastructure, and the revitalization of the economy. Reconstruction must be fully integrated into ongoing long-term development plans, taking account of future disaster risks. It must also consider the possibilities of reducing those risks by the incorporation of appropriate mitigation measures. Damaged structures and services may not necessarily be restored in their previous form or locations. It may include the replacement of any temporary arrangements established as a part of the emergency response or rehabilitation. Under conditions of conflict, however, rehabilitation and reconstruction may not be feasible. For obvious reasons of safety and security, activities in rehabilitation and reconstruction may need to wait until peace allows them.

1.5.2.1. Priorities and opportunities

The disaster occurred because the society was vulnerable to the impact of the hazard concerned. Rehabilitation and reconstruction must therefore not be seen as a process of simply restoring what existed previously. The need is rather to develop strategies and modalities to reconstitute services and renovate or replace essential structures such that vulnerability is reduced. These strategies must include long-term development policies and plans, which take account of the current situation including any basic changes resulting from the disaster. The disaster may, in fact, have created new opportunities for development by changing the environment and the point of departure, both in terms of physical structures and/or social patterns and attitudes. It will certainly have heightened awareness concerning disaster risks, and both the local populations and national authorities are likely to be especially receptive to proposals for risk reduction and preparedness measures. Such opportunities must be recognised and seized in the planning of rehabilitation and reconstruction projects, as well as in the formulation of new, long-term development programmes.

Assistance to rehabilitation and reconstruction must therefore be planned on the basis of a thorough assessment and appraisal of the technical and social issues involved. While the planning of such assistance cannot be unduly rushed, it must be accomplished as expeditiously as possible.

Seasonal factors must be considered and may determine the needed timetable for reconstruction, for example, the replacement of emergency shelter or the rehabilitation of irrigation systems in time for the next crop. The aim is to promote and assist recovery. Assistance during the post-disaster phase must be planned and implemented with this clearly in mind. Damaged structures and services which are essential to the society must be repaired or replaced, duly protected against future risks. At the same time, and no less important, ways must be found to help people recover, particularly those people who have the least resources to call on. As noted earlier, "the majority of people affected are the poor." For the poor, disasters represent lost property, jobs, and economic opportunity.

References

Alexander, D., *Natural Disasters*, London: Routledge, 2002.

.........., *Principles of Emergency planning and Management,* Harpended: Terra publishing, 2002.

Haddow, George D. and Jane A. Bullock, *Introduction to Emergency Management*, Amsterdam: Butterworth-Heinemann, 2003.

Quarantelli, E.L., *What is a disaster - Perspectives on the question*, New York: Routledge, 1998.

Wisner, B., P. Blaikie, T. Cannon, and I. Davis, *At Risk - Natural hazards, people's vulnerability and disasters*, Wiltshire: Routledge, 2004.

CHAPTER 2

Concept of Disaster Management

2.1. Introduction

A disaster is the product of a hazard such as earthquake, flood or windstorm coinciding with a vulnerable situation, which might include communities, cities or villages. There are several important characteristics that make Disasters different from Accidents. The loss of a sole income earner in a car crash may be a disaster to a family, but only an accident to the community.

Disaster can strike at any time-on a small or a large scale-but if an institution is prepared, the damage may be decreased or avoided. A disaster plan must be considered a living document. Its risk-assessment checklist must be periodically reviewed, its lists must be updated, and its collection priorities revised as needed. An effective disaster plan will do its best to insure that historical collections in our cultural institutions are safeguarded for the future.

Disaster management planning is complex; the written plan is the result of a wide range of preliminary activities. The entire process is most efficient if it is formally assigned to one person who acts as the disaster planner for the institution and is perhaps assisted by a planning team or committee. The institution's director may play this primary role or may delegate the responsibility, but it is important to remember that the process must be supported at the highest level of the organisation if it is to be effective. The planner should establish a timetable for the project and should define the scope and goals of the plan, which will depend largely on the risks faced by the institution.

2.2. Identifying Risks

A prudent first step is to list geographic and climatic hazards and other risks that could jeopardise the building and collections. These might include the institution's susceptibility to hurricanes, tornadoes, flash flooding, earthquakes, or forest fires, and even the possibility of unusual hazards such as volcanic eruptions. Consider man-made disasters such as power outages, sprinkler discharges, fuel or water supply failures, chemical spills, arson, bomb threats, or other such problems. Take note of the environmental risks that surround your institution.

Chemical industries, shipping routes for hazardous materials, and adjacent construction projects all expose the institution to damage. While all institutions are not vulnerable to all disasters, any event that is a real possibility should be covered under your emergency plan. Look carefully at your building and site. Check the surrounding terrain. Within the building, fire protection systems, electrical systems, plumbing, and environmental systems are of primary concern. Although there may be a wide range of disaster scenarios, the most common are water, fire, physical or chemical damage, or some combination of these. The specific procedures of a disaster plan focus on the prevention and mitigation of these types of damage.

2.2.1. Decreasing Risks

Once the institution's hazards are specified, the disaster planner should devise a programme with concrete goals, identifiable resources, and a schedule of activities for eliminating as many risks as possible. Geography and climate cannot be changed, but other vulnerabilities can be reduced. If building and collection conditions are regularly monitored, repaired and improved, many emergency situations will be eliminated. A regular programme of building inspection and maintenance should be a very high priority if one is not already in place.

It can prevent or reduce common emergencies resulting from burst pipes, defective climate-control equipment, worn electrical wiring, clogged drains, or other problems. If all improvements cannot be undertaken at once, make a schedule and follow it. If some items on your schedule prove impossible or are delayed, move on to the next goal and return to the earlier problem when it becomes more practical. Once building systems are in proper working order, devise a maintenance schedule.

Patchwork repairs and deferred maintenance only result in accelerated deterioration, leading to an increased risk of emergencies. Keep a log of building events like clogged drains, furnace cleaning, and equipment failures. The more you know about your building and its operation, the faster (and more economically) repairs can be made.

While water damage is the most common form of disaster for museums, every institution with collections of enduring value needs a good fire-protection system.

Since most emergencies seem to happen outside normal working hours, reliable fire detection systems on professional, twenty-four-hour monitors are a wise investment. Wherever possible, collections should also be protected by a fire-suppression system. The use of halon is no longer recommended. Preservation professionals now recommend wet-pipe sprinklers for most libraries and archives. In addition, water misting suppression systems have become available within the last several years; these can provide fire suppression using much less water than conventional sprinkler systems.

Before choosing a fire-protection system, be sure to contact a preservation professional or a fire-protection consultant for information about the latest developments in fire protection and for advice appropriate to your collections and situation. All fire-protection systems should be designed and installed by professionals with experience in servicing museums, archives, and libraries, because the needs of these institutions differ from the needs for home protection. Talk to colleagues at other local institutions or a preservation professional in your region for recommendations, and always check references.

Other actions that reduce building and collection vulnerability include maintaining a collection inventory, improving collection storage, and following good security and housekeeping procedures. An inventory will provide a basic list of holdings to assist in assigning priorities for salvage, and will be essential for insurance purposes. Improved collection storage, such as boxing and raising materials above the floor level, will reduce or eliminate damage when emergencies occur. Comprehensive security and housekeeping procedures will ward off emergencies such as theft, vandalism, and insect infestation. They will also ensure that fire exits are kept clear and fire hazards eliminated.

2.2.2. Cooperative Plan

Disaster planning should not take place in a vacuum. To work effectively, it must be integrated into the routine operating procedures of the institution. In fact, you will probably find that in planning for disasters you will also be working toward the accomplishment of other goals. For example, a properly functioning climate-control system will prevent fluctuations in temperature and relative humidity, resulting in a better preservation environment and a longer life for all collections. At the same time, this prevents disasters such as water leaks from air-handling units.

Similarly, if an institution surveys its collections and creates an inventory for disaster planning, a corollary benefit is better access to the collections for researchers and staff. Remember three important characteristics of an effective disaster plan: comprehensiveness, simplicity, and flexibility. The plan needs to address all types of emergencies and disasters that your institution is likely to face. It should include plans for both immediate response and long-term salvage and recovery efforts. Several national companies provide disaster-recovery services such as dehumidification and vacuum freeze-drying. Liaisons should be maintained with local emergency services so that they can respond appropriately in case of disaster.

2.3. Disaster Priorities

The first priority in any disaster is human safety. Saving collections is never worth endangering the lives of staff or patrons. In a major event, the fire department, civil defence authorities, or other professionals may restrict access to the building until it can be fully evaluated. Once safety concerns are met, the next consideration will be records and equipment crucial to the operation of the institution, such as registrar's records, inventories, and administrative files. Collections salvage and building rehabilitation will be the next priority.

Objects or collections of great importance to the institution must be identified ahead of time. If this is not done, valuable time may be wasted salvaging materials of little value or spent arguing about what should be saved first. Ideally, this step includes a floor plan that clearly states the priority of collections for salvage. This should be attached to the disaster plan, but the security of this type of information should be considered. It may be wise to allow only upper-level staff access to this part of the plan prior to an actual emergency.

The house built from cane and thatches that can be blown in a tropical cyclone are more vulnerable to the wind than a brick building. A badly constructed brick building is more likely to disintegrate with the violent ground shaking of an earthquake than cane or thatch hut and is more vulnerable to earthquake hazard.

Hence structures should be built strong enough to resist maximum force exerted by any event or for combination of event. Such measure will take care of the physical vulnerability. Social and economic conditions also determine the vulnerability of a society to an extent. It has been observed that human losses in disasters in developing countries like India tend to be high when compared to developed countries where material losses predominate.

2.4. Disaster Management Cycle

Disaster management can be defined as the body of policy and administrative decisions and operational activities which pertain to the various stages of a disaster at all levels. Broadly disaster management can be divided into pre-disaster and post-disaster contexts.

2.4.1. Tsunami

Tsunami is a Japanese word meaning "harbour wave". These waves, which often affect distant shores, originate from undersea or coastal seismic activity, landslides, and volcanic eruptions. Whatever the cause, sea water is displaced with a violent motion and swells up, ultimately surging over land with great destructive power.

2.4.1.1. Onset and causes

If the earthquake or under water land movement is near the coast then tsunami may strike suddenly and if the earth movement is far in the sea then it may take few minutes to hours before striking the coast. The onset is extensive and often very destructive. The general causes of Tsunamis are geological movements. It is produced in three major ways. The most common of these is fault movement on the sea floor, accompanied by an earthquake. To say that an earthquake causes a tsunami is not completely correct. Rather, both earthquakes and tsunamis result from fault movements. Probably the second most common cause of tsunamis is a landslide either occurring underwater or originating above the sea and then plunging into the water. The third major cause of tsunamis is volcanic activity. The flank of a volcano, located near the shore or underwater, may be uplifted or depressed similar to the action of a fault.

2.4.1.2. Warning

Tsunami is not a single giant wave. It consists of ten or more waves, which is termed as a "tsunami wave train." Since scientists cannot predict when earthquakes will occur, they cannot predict exactly when a tsunami will be generated. Studies of past historical tsunamis indicate where tsunamis are most likely to be generated, their potential heights, and flooding limits at specific coastal locations. With use of satellite technology it is possible to provide nearly immediate warnings of potentially tsunamigenic earthquakes. Warning time depends upon the distance of the epicenter from the coastline. The warning includes predicted times at selected coastal communities where the tsunami cold travel in a few hours. In case of tsunamigenic earthquakes or any other geological activity people near to the coastal areas may get very little time to evacuate on receiving of warning.

2.4.1.3. Elements at risk

All structures located within 200 m of the low-lying coastal area are most vulnerable to the direct impact of the tsunami waves as well as the impact of debris and boulders brought by it. Settlements in adjacent areas will be vulnerable to floods and scour. Structures constructed of wood, mud, thatch, sheets and structures without proper anchorage to foundations are liable to be damaged by tsunami waves and flooding.

Other elements at risk are infrastructure facilities like ports & harbours, telephone and electricity poles, cables. Ships and fishing boats/nets near the coast also add to the destruction caused by tsunami waves.

2.4.1.4. Typical effects

Physical damage: Local tsunami events or those less than 30 minutes from the source cause the majority of damage. The force of can raze everything in its path. It is the flooding effect of a tsunami, however, that most greatly effects human settlements by water damage to homes and businesses, roads, bridges and other infrastructure. Ships, port facilities, boats/trawlers, fishing nets also get damaged.

Environmental damage: There is evidence of ever increasing impact upon the environment on account of the effects of tsunamis. The range varies from generation of tonnes of debris on account of structural collapse of weaker buildings, release of toxic chemicals into the environment on account of chemical leak/spillage/process failure/utility breakages/ collateral hazards and negative impact on the already fragile ecosystems.

Casualties and public health: Deaths occur principally from drowning as water inundates homes or neighbourhoods. Many people may be washed out to sea or crushed by the giant waves. There may be some injuries from battering by debris and wounds may become contaminated.

Water supply: sewage pipes may be damaged causing major sewage disposal problems. Drinking water shortage arises due to breakage of water mains and contamination. Open wells and ground water may become unfit for drinking due to contamination of salt water and debris.

Standing Crops and food supplies: flooding by tsunami causes damage to the standing crops and also to the food supplies in the storage facilities. The land may be rendered infertile due to salt-water incursion from the sea.

2.4.1.5. Specific preparedness measures

Hazard mapping—a hazard map should be prepared with designated areas expected to be damaged by flooding by tsunami waves. Historical data could be of help ion showing areas inundated in the past. Keeping in mind the vulnerable areas, evacuation routes should be constructed and mapped. The plan should be followed by evacuation drill.

Early warning systems—a well-networked system in place can warn the communities of the coastal areas when the threat is perceived. Tsunami warning should be disseminated to local, state, national as well as the international community so as to be prepared as they are capable of crossing across continents. The information can be broadcasted to the local emergency officers and the general public. On receiving of the warning the action should be to evacuate the place as decided in the evacuation plan.

Community preparedness—communities in the coastal areas are faced by the wrath of cyclones, storm surge and tsunami waves. It is important that the community is better prepared to take suitable actions on receiving of the threat and follow emergency evacuation plans and procedures. A community, which chooses to ignore warning, may get severely affected if they are not prepared to take immediate measures.

2.4.1.6. Mitigation strategies

Site planning and land management—Within the broader framework of a comprehensive plan, site planning determines the location, configuration, and density of development on particular sites and is, therefore, an important tool in reducing tsunami risk.

2.4.2. Landslides

Landslides are slippery masses of rock, earth or debris, which move by force of their own weight down mountain slopes or river banks.

2.4.2.1. Onset and warning

Though they occur gradually, however sudden failure (sliding) can occur without warning. They may take place in combination with earthquakes, floods and volcanoes. There are no clearly established warnings in place indicating occurrence of landslide and hence difficult to predict the actual occurrence. Areas of high risk can be determined by use of information on geology, hydrology, vegetation cover, past occurrence and consequences in the region.

2.4.2.2. Causes

Geological Weak material: weathered materials, jointed or fissured materials, contrast in permeability and contrast in stiffness (stiff, dense material over plastic materials).

Erosion: Wave erosion of slope toe, glacial erosion of slope toe, subterranean erosion (Deposition loading slope or its crest, Vegetation removal.

Intense rainfall: Storms that produce intense rainfall for periods as short as several hours or have a more moderate intensity lasting several days have triggered abundant landslides. Human Excavation of slope and its toe, Loading of slope/toe, draw down in reservoir, mining, deforestation, irrigation, vibration/blast, Water leakage from services.

Earthquake shaking has triggered landslides in many different topographic and geologic settings. Rock falls, soil slides and rockslides from steep slopes involving relatively thin or shallow dis-aggregated soils or rock, or both have been the most abundant types of landslides triggered by historical earthquakes. Volcanic eruption Deposition of loose volcanic ash on hillsides commonly is followed by accelerated erosion and frequent mud or debris flows triggered by intense rainfall.

2.4.2.3. Elements at risk

The most common elements at risk are the settlements built on the steep slopes, built at the toe and those built at the mouth of the streams emerging from the mountain valley. All those buildings constructed without appropriate foundation for a given soil and in sloppy areas are also at risk. Roads, communication line and buried utilities are vulnerable.

2.4.2.4. Indian landslides

Landslide constitute a major natural hazard in India country, which accounts for considerable loss of life and damage to communication routes, human settlements, agricultural fields and forest lands. The Indian subcontinent, with diverse physiographic, seismotectonic and climatological conditions is subjected to varying degree of landslide hazards; the Himalayas including Northeastern mountains ranges being the worst affected, followed by a section of Western Ghats and the Vindhyas. Removal of vegetation and toe erosion have also triggered slides Torrential monsoon on the vegetation cover removed slopes was the main causative factors in the Peninsular India namely in Western Ghat and Nilgiris.

2.4.2.5. Typical effects

Physical damage: Landslides destroy anything that comes in their path. They block or bury roads, lines of communication, settlements, river flow, agricultural land, etc. It also includes loss to agricultural production and land area. In addition physical effects such as flooding may also occur.

2.4.2.6. Community-based mitigation

The most damaging landslides are often related to human intervention such as construction of roads, housing and other infrastructure in vulnerable slopes and regions. Other community-based activities that can mitigate landslides are education and awareness generation among the communities, establishing community based monitoring, timely warning and evacuation system. Communities can play a vital role in identifying the areas where there is land instability. Compacting ground locally, slope stabilization, and avoiding construction of houses in hazardous locations are something that the community has to agree and adhere to avoid damage from the possible landslides. This would also reduce the burden of shifting of settlements from hazardous slopes and rebuild in safe site as it is less practical to do in large scale.

2.4.3. Cyclones

Cyclone is a violent storm, often of vast extent, characterised by high winds rotating about a calm center of low atmospheric pressure. This center moves onward, often with a velocity of 50km an hour.

2.4.3.1. Onset type

They strike suddenly although it takes time to build up. They can be tracked on the development but accurate landfall is predictable barely few hours. The onset is extensive and often very destructive.

2.4.3.2. Warning

Low pressure and the development can be detected hours or days before its damage effects start. Satellite tracking can track the movement since the build up and the likely path is projected. Warning and evacuation is done along the projected path. It is difficult to predict the accuracy. Accurate landfall predictions can give only a few hours' notice to threatened populations. In addition, people generally opt to wait until the very last minute before abandoning their home and possessions. Deaths from drowning in the high tides and sudden flooding and material losses are therefore often very high. The India Meteorological Department (IMD) issues warning against severe weather phenomena like tropical cyclones, heavy rains and snow, cold and heat waves, etc., which cause destruction of life and property. Cyclone warning is disseminated by several means such as satellite based disaster warning systems, radio, television, telephone, fax, high priority telegram, public announcements and bulletins in press. Advancement in Information Technology in the form of Internet, Geograhical Information System (GIS), Remote Sensing, Satellite communication, etc. can help a great deal in planning and implementation of hazards reduction schemes.

2.4.3.3. Elements at risk

All lightweight structures and those built of mud, wood, older buildings with weak walls and structures without proper anchorage to the foundations will be at great risk. Settlements located in low-lying coastal areas will be vulnerable to the direst effects of the cyclones such as wind, rain and storm surge. Settlements in adjacent areas will be vulnerable to floods, mudslides or landslides due to heavy rains. Other elements at risk are fences, telephone and electricity poles, cables, light elements of structures -roofs, signboards, hoardings, coconut crowns, fishing boats and large trees.

2.4.3.4. *Typical effects*

First, in a sudden, brief onslaught, high winds cause major damage to infrastructure and housing, in particular fragile constructions. They are generally followed by heavy rains and floods and, in flat coastal areas by storm surge riding on tidal waves and inundating the land over long distances of even upto 15km inland.

Physical damage: structures will be damaged or destroyed by the wind force, flooding and storm surge. Light pitched roofs of most structures especially the ones fitted on to industrial buildings will suffer severe damage.

Casualties and public heath: caused by flooding and flying elements, contamination of water supplies may lead to viral outbreaks, diarrhea, and malaria.

Water supplies: Ground and piped water supply may get contaminated by floodwaters.

Crops and food supplies: High winds and rains will ruin the standing crop and food stock lying in low lying areas. Plantation type crops such as banana and coconut are extremely vulnerable. Salt from the sea water may be deposited on the agricultural land and increase the salinity. The loss of the crop may lead to acute food shortage.

Communication: Severe disruption in the communication links as the wind may bring down the electricity and communication towers, electricity and telephone poles, telephone lines, antennas and satellite disk and broadcasting services. Transport lines (road and rail) may be curtailed. Relief materials may not reach the affected site.

2.4.3.5. *Potential for reducing hazard*

Coastal belt plantation (green belt plantation along the coastal line in a scientific interweaving pattern) can reduce the effect of the hazard. Providing a cover through green belt sustains less damage. Forests act as a wide buffer zone against strong winds and flash floods. Without the forest the cyclone travel freely inland. The lack of protective forest cover allows water to inundate large areas and cause destruction. With the loss of the forest cover each consecutive cyclone can penetrate further inland. Flood protection measures can be taken to reduce the impact of flood hazards.

2.4.3.6. Main mitigation strategies

Hazard mapping - Meteorological records of the wind speed and the directions give the probability of the winds in the region. Cyclones can be predicted several days in advance. The onset is extensive and often very destructive. Past records and paths can give the pattern of occurrence for particular wind speeds. A hazard map will illustrate the areas vulnerable to the cyclone in any given year. It will be useful to estimate the severity of the cyclone and various damage intensities in the region. The map is prepared with data inputs of past climatological records, history of wind speed, frequency of flooding etc.

Land use control designed so that least critical activities are placed in vulnerable areas. Location of settlements in the flood plains is at utmost risk. Siting of key facilities must be marked in the land use. Policies should be in place to regulate land use and enforcement of building codes. Vulnerable areas should be kept for parks, grazing or play grounds.

Engineered structures: Structures need to be built to withstand wind forces. Good site selection is also important. Majority of the buildings in coastal areas are built with locally available materials and have no engineering inputs.

2.4.4. Floods

Flood is a temporary inundation of large regions as the result of an increase in reservoir, or of rivers flooding their banks because of heavy rains, high winds, cyclones, storm surge along coast, tsunami, melting snow or dam bursts.

2.4.4.1. Onset type

Floods may happen gradually and take hours, or can even happen suddenly due to breach of the structures, spillover etc. heavy downpour can cause flash floods in the region.

Flood forecasting and warning has become highly developed in the past two decades. With the advancement in the technology such as satellite and remote-sensing equipments flood waves can be tracked as they move downwards. Except for flash floods there is usually a reasonable warning period. Heavy precipitation will give sufficient warning of the coming river flood. High tides with high winds may indicate flooding in the coastal areas. Evacuation is possible with suitable monitoring and warning.

Flash floods defined as floods which occurs within six hours of the beginning of heavy rainfall, and are usually associated with cloud bursts, storms and cyclones requiring rapid localized warnings and immediate response if damage is to be mitigated. Wireless network and telephone connections are used to monitor flood conditions. In case of flash floods, warnings for timely evacuation may not always be possible.

2.4.4.2. Elements at risk

Anything in the flood plains will get inundated. Buildings built of earth, weak foundations and water soluble materials will collapse endangering humans and their property. Basements of buildings are under risk. Utilities such as sewerage, water supply, communication lines, and power are put at risk. Food stock in the godowns, agricultural fields, salt pans, livestock, vehicles, machinery and equipments mounted on the ground, fishing boats are also put at risk.

2.4.4.3. Indian floods

Floods occur in almost all rivers basins of the country. Heavy rainfall, inadequate capacity of rivers to carry the high flood discharge, inadequate drainage to carry away the rainwater quickly to Streams/Rivers are the main causes of floods. Ice jams or land slides blocking streams; typhoons and cyclones also cause floods. Excessive rainfall combined with inadequate carrying capacity of streams resulting in over spilling of banks is the cause for flooding in majority of cases. Rashtriya Barh Ayog (RBA) constituted by the Government of India in 1976 carried out an extensive analysis to estimate the flood affected area in the country.

2.4.4.4. Hazard zones

The Vulnerability Atlas of India shows pictorially the areas liable to floods. The flood hazard map is based on the Flood Atlas of India brought out by the Central Water Commission, state wise marking both the areas which are liable to flooding as well as those which have been protected. The maps given in the Vulnerability Atlas of India show the district boundaries and the location of the district towns along with the rivers district wise identification of vulnerable areas will be easy. Besides the problems of flooding in the river plains, heavy intensity rains could cause local; flooding in certain areas where the drainage is either naturally poor or the drains are choked due to various reasons such as careless dumping of refuse in the drains and lack of maintenance. Much of the flooding in the towns and cities occur due to such cases. Under cyclonic winds in coastal areas, the sea coast of India can be flooded due to heavy down pour on the one hand and storm surge on the other. The depth of inland water inundation could be worked out by taking the storm surge heights.

2.4.4.5. Potential for reducing hazard

Embankments along the rivers, sea walls along the coasts may keep water away from the flood plains. Water flow can be regularized through construction of the reservoirs, check dams, alternate drainage channels/routes, increasing vegetation cover and by providing storm drains.

2.4.4.6. Mitigation strategies

Mapping of the flood prone areas is a primary step involved in reducing the risk of the region. Historical records give the indication of the flood inundation areas and the period of occurrence and the extent of the coverage. The basic map is combined with other maps and data to form a complete image of the floodplain. Warning can be issued looking into the earlier marked heights of the water levels in case of potential threat. In the coastal areas the tide levels and the land characteristics will determine the submergence areas. Flood hazard mapping will give the proper indication of water flow during floods.

Land use control will reduce danger of life and property when waters inundate the floodplains and the coastal areas. The number of casualties is related to the population in the area at risk. It's better to reduce the densities in areas where neighborhoods are to be developed. In areas where people already have built their settlements, measures should be taken to relocate to better sites so as to reduce vulnerability. No major development should be permitted in the areas, which are subjected to high flooding. Important facilities should be built in safe areas. In urban areas, water-holding areas can be created in ponds, lakes or low-lying areas. Construction of engineered structures in the flood plains and strengthening of structures to withstand flood forces and seepage. The buildings should be constructed on an elevated area.

Flood Control aims to reduce flood damage. This can be done by Flood Reduction by decreasing the amount of runoff by treatment like reforestation, protection of vegetation, clearing of debris from streams and other water holding areas, conservation of ponds and lakes etc. Flood Diversion includes levees, embankments, dams and channel improvement. Dams can store water and can release water at a manageable rate. But failure of dams in earthquakes and operation of releasing the water can cause floods in the lower areas. Flood Proofing reduces the risk of damage. Measures include use of sand bags to keep floodwater away, blocking or sealing of doors and windows of houses etc. Houses may be elevated by building on raised land. Buildings should be constructed away from water bodies.

2.4.4.7. Community based mitigation

Sedimentation clearance, reforestation programme, dike and flood wall construction can be taken as part of the community based mitigation programme. The community can participate in flood fighting by organising work parties to repair embankments, pile sandbags and stockpile needed materials. Farming practices have to be flood compatible. Special varieties of seeds are available which can be harvested during the flood season. Houses constructed need to be flood resistant and multipurpose shelter should be constructed by the community. Banks of the earth can be raised and it can give shelter to the community as well as the livestock during the time of floods.

2.4.5. Drought

Drought is an insidious natural hazard that results from a departure of precipitation from expected or normal that, when extended over a season or longer period of time, is insufficient to meet the demands of human, plant and animal activities.

2.4.5.1. Onset type and warning

Drought is a slow-onset disaster and as it is difficult to demarcate the time of its onset and end. Falling rainfall levels, falling groundwater levels, drying wells, rivers and reservoirs, and poor agricultural production warn the onset of drought. According to the Indian Meteorological Department, the country is said to be drought affected when the overall rainfall deficiency is more than 10 per cent of the long period average and more than 20 per cent of the country area is affected by such drought conditions.

2.4.5.2. Elements at risk

Drought impacts mostly rainfed crops to start with and subsequently the irrigated crops. Areas with minimum of alternative water sources to rainfall (ground and canal water supplies), areas subjected to drastic environmental degradation such as denuded forest lands and altered ecosystems, and areas where livelihoods alternative to agriculture are least developed are most vulnerable to drought. The herdsman, landless laborers, subsistence farmers, the women, children, and farm animals are the most vulnerable groups affected by the drought conditions.

2.4.5.3. Typical effects

Drought, different from other natural disasters, do not cause any structural damages. The typical effects include loss of crop, dairy, timber (forest fires), and fishery production; increase in energy demand for pumping water; reduced energy production; increased unemployment, loss of biodiversity, reduced water, air, and landscape quality; groundwater depletion, food shortage, health reduction and loss of life, increased poverty, reduced quality of life, and social unrest leading to migration.

2.4.5.4. Mitigation strategies

Drought monitoring is continuous observation of rainfall situation, water availability in reservoirs, lakes, rivers and comparing with the existing water needs of various sectors of the society. Water supply augmentation and conservation through rainwater harvesting in houses and farmers' fields increases the content of water available. Water harvesting by either allowing the runoff water from all the fields to a common point or allowing it to infiltrate into the soil where it has fallen help increase water availability for sustained agricultural production. Expansion of irrigation facilities reduces the drought vulnerability. Land use based on its capability helps in optimum use of land and water and can avoid the undue demand created due to their misuse. Livelihood planning identifies those livelihoods which are least affected by the drought. Some of such livelihoods include increased off-farm employment opportunities, collection of non-timber forest produce from the community forests, raising goats, and carpentry etc.

2.4.5.5. Drought planning

The basic goal of drought planning is to improve the effectiveness of preparedness and response efforts by enhancing monitoring, mitigation and response measures. Planning would help in effective coordination among state and national agencies in dealing with the drought. Components of drought plan include establishing drought taskforce which is a team of specialists who can advise the government in taking decision to deal with drought situation, establishing coordination mechanism among various agencies which deal with the droughts, providing crop insurance schemes to the farmers to cope with the drought related crop losses, and public awareness generation.

2.4.5.6. Public awareness and education

Educating the masses on various strategies include organising drought information meetings for the public and media, implementing water conservation awareness programs in the mass media like television, publishing and distributing pamphlets on water conservation techniques and agricultural drought management strategies like crop contingency plans and rainwater harvesting and establishing drought information centers for easy access to the farmers.

2.4.6. Forest Fire

Forest Fire/Wild Fire is one of the destructive natural forces known to mankind. While sometimes caused by lightning, nine out of ten wildfires are human-caused. "Wild Fire" is the term applied to any unwanted and unplanned fire burning in forest, shrub or grass.

In India there are very few cases of fire due to natural causes. The majority of the forest fires (99 percent) in the country are human caused. It is widely acknowledged that most of these fires are caused by the people deliberately and have a close relationship to their socio-economic conditions. Grazing, shifting cultivation, and collection of minor forest products by villagers are major causes of fires in India. Carelessness of the picnickers, travellers, and campers are also responsible for forest fires.

2.4.6.1. Operational fire management systems

The central and state governments in the country are enabled to legislate on forestry issues. The implementation part of the forest policy/programmes lies with the state government. Thus, fire prevention, detection, and suppression activities are the responsibility of the state governments' forestry departments. The policy, planning, and financing are the primary responsibility of the Central Government. There is generally no separate department for carrying out forest fire management in the states. The regular staff of the forest departments in the states carries out various activities of forest fire management. During forest fire seasons in some of the divisions, firewatchers are recruited by the state governments as a special provision. At the central level, the Ministry of Environment and Forests is the ministry responsible for forest conservation and protection. Forest fire management is administered by the "Forest Protection Division" of the Ministry, which is headed by a Deputy Inspector General of Forests. The Ministry is implementing a plan called "Modern Forest Fire Control Methods" in India under which state governments are provided financial assistance for fire prevention and control. This assistance is being used by the state governments for procuring hand tools, fire resistant clothes, firefighting tools, radios, fire watch towers, fire finders, creation of fire lines, research, training, and In India, Joint Forest Management (JFM) Committees have been established at the village level to involve people in forest protection and conservation.

2.4.6.2. Public policies concerning fire

India's National Forest Policy (1988) presents a visionary strategy for forest conservation and management and emphasises protection of forests against encroachment, fire, and grazing. It states that "The incidence of forest fires in the country is high. Standing trees and fodder are destroyed on a large scale and natural regeneration annihilated by such fires. Special precautions should be taken during the fire season. Improved and modern management practices should be adopted to deal with forest fire." This policy provides a positive step towards protection of forests from fire. The legal and policy framework exists in support of fire protection in the country.

2.4.6.3. Role of education

A lack of understanding of the value of the wildlife reserves among most local people and their consequent hostility towards reserve protection and law enforcement are identified as a major problem to be addressed at most wildlife reserves in India. Arson by local people is a frequent form of backlash against law enforcement by park staff in national parks and wildlife sanctuaries in India. Such hostility makes law enforcement difficult and often renders the reserve staff ineffective.

2.4.6.4. Needs of fire management

The incidence of forest fires in the country is on the increase and more area is burned each year. The major cause of this failure is the piecemeal approach to the problem. Both the national focus and the technical resources required for sustaining a systematic forest fire management programme are lacking in the country. Important forest fire management elements like strategic fire centres, coordination among Ministries, funding, human resource development, fire research, fire detection system by using satellite images, fire management, and extension programmes are missing. Taking into consideration the serious nature of the problem, it is necessary to make some major improvements in the forest fire management strategy for the country.

2.4.7. Epidemic

An epidemic is defined as the occurrence of an illness or other health-related event that is clearly in excess of unexpected occurrence.

2.4.7.1. Onset type and warning

The onset of an epidemic can be either rapid or sudden and this depends on several factors. An epidemic can be anticipated by the rise in number of people suffering from a particular disease. In some cases an epidemic can be anticipated or predicted by an increase in the vector breading sites or in the death of the disease carriers.

A disease epidemic or outbreak is the occurrence of cases of a particular disease in excess of the expected, therefore, demanding that emergency control measures be implemented. The threat of communicable disease outbreaks is greater after a disaster than in non-emergency situations, particularly when large populations have been displaced. However, an epidemic or outbreak will only occur if the equilibrium between the population's susceptibility, the virulence of the infectious agent (bacteria, viruses, parasites, or fungi or their products) and the environment that promotes the exposure is upset.

2.4.7.2. Causes

The main cause for an epidemic is the pathogen (virus, bacteria, protozoa or rarely fungi). Reports of outbreaks of communicable diseases are increasing in number and reported in many of the national dailies. This is because of a number of reasons. For instance poor sanitary conditions may contaminate food and water and also suffice the environment for breeding conditions for the vector. Other factors include the seasonal changes that favour the breeding of an insect vector such as mosquito in the rainy season, exposure of non-immune persons say tourists and migrants, poverty, overcrowding etc.

Poverty is one of the major factor contributing to the vulnerability. Impact of natural disasters on the environment also leads to outbreak of epidemic. Part of the increase in the number of outbreaks is due to exposure of unreported cases of diseases as a result of better reporting and increased coverage of health services.

2.4.7.3. Typical effects

Epidemics cause illness and death. There are other secondary effects such as disruption in the society and economic losses. Vulnerability is high among those are poorly nourished, people living in unhygienic sanitary conditions, poor water supply, individuals who do not have an access to the health services or those who have weak immune systems. The outbreak of an epidemic in situations where already a natural calamity has struck will cause life threatening situations.

2.4.7.4. Potential risk reduction measures

Structuring the health services is important to have clear understanding of roles and responsibilities of the public health system. Organisational preparedness and the coordination mechanism is required right from the State and District to the sub center level which is manned by the Village Health Nurses or the Health Workers.

Contingency Plan for response should be prepared after identifying the epidemics that are likely to occur in the region. Early warning system through a surveillance system is the primary requirement so as to have an effective response and prevent any outbreaks. For this, surveillance need to be carried out at a regular basis through the routine surveillance system by involving the health tier system. Maps of all the health facilities in the region with an inventory of drugs and vaccines, laboratory set ups, list of number of doctors and supporting staff etc. need to be kept ready and updated at regular intervals.

Training need to be given to so as to build the capacity at all levels. Training will help to cope better during the emergency response period for epidemics. Personnel protection through vaccination is an effective mitigation strategy and will protect the persons at risk.

Common sources of infection carriers can be tackled by many measures. Strategies included are improving the sanitary conditions, drive to check and fumigate breeding places of any vector (source of infection), improving disposal methods of waste, disinfecting the water source etc.

2.4.8. Heatwave

Heatwave is a complex phenomenon resulting from a certain combination of temperature, humidity, air movement and duration. Simply stated, a heatwave is an extended period of very high summer temperatures with the potential to adversely affect communities.

2.4.8.1. Heatwave dangers and effects

Human effects: in many parts of the country and the world, every summer thousands of people suffer from heat stress when the bodies absorb more heat than they can dispel. Unless prompt preventive/treatment is received, they suffer the serious or even fatal consequences of heat stroke. Regardless of these statistics, heat wave is probably the most under-rated of all natural hazards. The level of discomfort experienced in warm, moist tropical and sub-tropical conditions is determined by a range of climatic variables, principally air temperature, humidity and wind; as well as cultural variables including clothing, occupation and accommodation; and physiological variables such as health, fitness, age and the level of becoming accustomed.

2.4.8.2. Community awareness

There appears to be a significant lack of community awareness of the risks associated with heat wave, even though several parts of the country experience such events with some regularity. It is a widely overlooked, even unknown, killer. It is ideal to create awareness among the communities and ask them to take suitable precautionary steps during the peak summer months. Media and Community education can be launched prior to the onset of the heatwave conditions. Fires are very dangerous. It is an event of something burning and is often destructive taking up toll of life and property. It is observed that more people die in fires than in cyclones, earthquakes, floods and all other natural disasters combined. The most common human-caused hazard is fire in large occupied buildings and in slums built of combustible materials. Causes can be accidental or deliberate, but unless structures are built to safe fire standards as mentioned in the National Building Code, and sound emergency procedures are used, heavy loss of life can result. While no country in the world is entirely safe, lack of capacity to limit the impact of hazards remains a major burden for developing countries.

The true costs of disasters, taking into account less quantifiable effects such as the loss of personal belongings or jobs, widening trade or government budget deficits, or the increasing scale and depth of poverty, are even higher.

Vulnerability to disasters is a function of human action and behavior. It describes the degree to which a socio-economic system or physical assets are either susceptible or resilient to the impact of natural hazards. It is determined by a combination of several factors, including awareness of hazards, the condition of human settlements and infrastructure, public policy and administration, the wealth of a given society and organised abilities in all fields of disaster and risk management. Lack of awareness among the public and decision-makers about factors and human activities that contribute to environmental degradation and disaster vulnerability are aggravating these trends.

There is a close correlation between the trends of increased demographic pressure especially in developing countries, and particularly in least developed countries, escalated environmental degradation, increased human vulnerability and the intensity of the impact of hazards. For example, river and lake floods are aggravated or even caused by deforestation, which causes erosion and clogs rivers, siltation of riverbeds and other factors.

Poverty and hazard vulnerability is integrally linked and mutually reinforcing. The accelerated, and often uncontrolled, growth of cities has contributed to the ecological transformation of their immediate surroundings (pressure on scarce land, deforestation, etc.) In addition, the lack of appropriate drainage systems and/or sealing (use of concrete and asphalt) increase the volume and speed of rainfall runoff thus making many cities more vulnerable to flash floods. Recent catastrophic earthquakes highlight other key deficiencies and trends in the approach to disaster risk reduction, such as a poor understanding by decision makers of seismic related risk, as well as the tendency of some builders, to use the cheapest designs and construction materials to increase short-term economic returns on their investment.

2.5. Impact of Disaster on Economic Loss

Economic losses are often reported with reference to only the direct losses from infrastructure and assets destroyed during large-scale disasters. They seldom take into account the economic implications of reduced levels of production linked to damage in productive assets or infrastructure that in turn access to raw materials, energy labour or markets. The use of economic loss indicator of disaster impact on development varies for different natural hazards.

Disasters can wipe out the grains of economic development. Catastrophic disasters result in the destruction of fixed assets and physical capital, interruption of production and trade, diversion and depletion of savings and public and private investment. While absolute level of economic loss are greater in developed countries due to the far higher density and cost of infrastructure and production levels, less developed countries suffer higher levels of relative loss when seen as a proportion of Gross Domestic Product (GDP).

At the local level, disasters can seriously impact household livelihoods and push already vulnerable groups into poverty. The loss of income earners, through death or injury, the interruption of production or access to markets and the destruction of productive assets, such as home-based workshops, are all examples of ways in which disasters affect local and household economies. The capacity of a household or local community to absorb the impact and recover from a major natural hazard will be seriously limited if already weakened overtime by a series of smaller-scale losses.

A population that has weakened and depleted by natural disaster, particularly when it coincides with losses from malnutrition etc., will be less likely to have the organizational capacity to maintain irrigation works, bunds in fields for water harvesting, hill slope terraces, shelter belts. Without these social assets communities become more vulnerable.

In addition to the loss of social assets themselves, there are many examples of disaster events destroying the gains of the health, sanitation, drinking water, housing and education sectors that underpin social development. Women suffer additional stresses in disaster situations and also bear a disproportionate burden of the additional domestic & income-generating work necessary for survival following a disaster event. When women are exposed to additional stresses, the level of social development is reduced.

In rural programmes and drought prone areas, specific regard should be given to food-security and promotion of agriculture techniques and inter-cropping that reduce hazard-related agriculture losses. Disaster reduction policies and measures need to be implemented, with a two-fold aim: to enable societies to be resilient to natural hazards while ensuring that development efforts do not increase the vulnerability to these hazards. Disaster risk management falls under global trends of causing policymakers to rethink the institutional setup of governments, and the roles and responsibilities of different levels of government in achieving developmental objectives.

References

Alexander, D., *Natural Disasters,* London: UCL Press, 1993.

Albala-Bertrand, J.M., *Political economy of large natural disasters: with special reference to developing countries,* Oxford: Clarendon Press, 1993.

Allen, E., "Political Responses to Flood Disaster: The Case of Rio De Janeiro", 1988, In A. Varley (Ed.) *Disasters, Development and the Environment.* London: Belhaven, 1994.

Berke, P., Kartez, J. and Wenger, D., "Recovery after Disaster: Achieving Sustainable Development, Mitigation and Equity", *Disasters,* 1993.

Cannon, T., "Vulnerability Analysis and the Explanation of 'Natural' Disasters", In Varley, A. (Ed.) *Disasters, Development and the Environment:* 13-30, London: Belhaven Press, 1994.

Parker, D. (Ed.), *Floods,* 2 vols., London: Routledge, 2000.

Seaman, J., Leivesley, S. and Hogg, C., *Epidemiology of Natural Disasters,* Basel: Karger, 1984.

CHAPTER 3

Disaster Preparedness

3.1. Introduction

Disaster preparedness involves forecasting and taking precautionary measures prior to an imminent threat when advance warnings are possible. Preparedness planning improves the response to the effects of a disaster by organising the delivery of timely and effective rescue, relief and assistance. Preparedness involves the development and regular testing of warning systems and plans for evacuation or other measures to be taken during a disaster alert period to minimise potential loss of life and physical damage. It also involves the education and training of officials and the population at risk, the training of intervention teams, and the establishment of policies, standards, organisational arrangements and operational plans to be applied following a disaster. Effective plans also consider securing resources, possibly including stockpiling supplies and earmarking funds. These plans must be supported by enabling legislation.

Disaster preparedness minimises the adverse effects of a hazard through effective precautionary actions, rehabilitation and recovery to ensure the timely, appropriate and effective organisation and delivery of relief and assistance following a disaster.

Long-term risk reduction measures are intended to minimise the adverse effects of a hazard by eliminating the vulnerabilities, which hazards would otherwise expose. These measures directly reduce the potential impact of a hazard before it strikes. Disaster preparedness assumes that certain groups of people or property will nevertheless remain vulnerable, and that preparedness will have to address the consequences of a disaster's impact. Too often the end product of disaster preparedness is seen as a static plan to be devised and then field until it is needed. Disaster preparedness must be seen as an active, on-going process. Preparedness plans are dynamic ventures, which need to be reviewed, modified, updated and tested on a regular basis.

Some analysts distinguish between "active" and "passive" disaster preparedness measures. Passive aspects of disaster preparedness include the preparation of disaster manuals, stockpiling of relief goods and the development of computer lists of resources and personnel. "Active" disaster preparedness would include developing comprehensive response plans, monitoring hazard threats, training emergency personnel, and training members of the communities at risk.

Disaster management involves the response to or anticipation of a hazardous event. Disaster mitigation includes both disaster preparedness and prevention. One of the most difficult aspects of disaster management is that of timing. Timing is also critical to disaster preparedness. Speed and timeliness are often treated synonymously, causing serious problems in the relationship between relief inputs and their effects. There are certain basic needs in some types of disasters, such as shelter and clothing that may be required immediately. In terms of alleviating immediate distress, speed will be essential. However, there are other forms of relief that, under certain circumstances, may be disruptive unless delayed. There is the obvious example of food. Rushing in excessive amounts of food aid before a clear assessment of local market conditions and agricultural prospects are known can create dependency and undermine local economies. Timeliness, not speed, should be the preparedness criterion. Appropriate assistance requires careful scrutiny. The list of inappropriate relief items that find their way to disaster-affected communities is all too long. The issue goes beyond the standard stories of canned ham sent to nonpork eating communities and spiked-heeled women's shoes sent to flooded regions.

The effective organisation and delivery of the disaster response suggest obvious criteria for disaster preparedness. Inevitably, disaster situations create conditions of chaos. The best-laid plans can reduce, but not eliminate, that chaos. Effectiveness is relative. Preparedness plans should seek to anticipate the sources of chaos and should tell us what to do when plans go awry. The criterion of effectiveness becomes particularly important in the context of distribution. The key here is that effectiveness is measured in terms of the ability to deliver needed relief to those in need. Often in emergency situations, food and non-food relief arrives at the scene of a disaster without a pre-established structure to ensure that those in greatest need are the immediate beneficiaries. The most important test of effectiveness is that those in need receive adequate relief and assistance.

3.2. Disaster Contingency Plans

Vulnerability analysis is a continuing, dynamic process of people and organisations assessing the hazards and risks they face and determining what they wish to do about them, if anything. Vulnerability assessment also includes a means of structured data collection geared towards understanding the levels of potential threats, needs and immediately available resources. Assessment includes two general categories of information. The first is relatively static infrastructure information that provides bases for determining the extent of development, types of physical advantages and disadvantages faced by communities residing in an area, and a "map" of available structures that might be useful in times of emergencies. The other category includes relatively dynamic socioeconomic data indicating causes and levels of vulnerability, demographic shifts and types of economic activity.

Planning is the theme of the whole disaster preparedness exercise. One objective is to have agreed-upon, implementable plans in place, for which commitment and resources are relatively assured. Planning for readiness includes working out agreements between people or agencies as to who will provide services in an emergency to ensure an effective, coordinated response. These agreements might take various forms: memos of understanding, mutual aid agreements, or individual agency and master plans. The ultimate objective is not to write a plan but to stimulate on-going interactions between parties, which may result in written, usable agreements. The written plan is a product, but not the main goal, of the planning process. There are four obvious points to be considered in any planning effort.

Disaster contingency plans normally focus on means to address particular hazards. This is not to say that a good contingency plan ignores the need for mitigation and recovery measures, but it usually is not concerned with the entire disaster continuum, such as rehabilitation and development linkages. The main focus is on ways to address a particular hazard, within a fairly finite period, such as from early warning and response to immediate recovery phases. An effective national strategy will usually generate various contingency plans to meet specific disaster conditions.

Disasters strike in different ways and at different times. For example, certain countries have to face persistent, slow-onset disasters that occur almost on an annual basis during a three to five year cycle, affecting substantial portions of a society, such as drought-related famines in the Horn of Africa. Other countries face chronic sudden-onset threats. For example, floods in Bangladesh may normally affect a predictable part of the population in a geographically well-defined area. There are other nations, including Mexico, which may suffer severely from natural disasters, which are relatively rare in occurrence, spread out over much longer intervals. The answer to what types of plans or strategies are needed obviously depends on these and other variables.

Disaster contingency plans normally focus on means to address particular hazards. This is not to say that a good contingency plan ignores the need for mitigation and recovery measures, but it usually is not concerned with the entire disaster continuum, such as rehabilitation and development linkages. The main focus is on ways to address a particular hazard, within a fairly finite period, such as from early warning and response to immediate recovery phases. An effective national strategy will usually generate various contingency plans to meet specific disaster conditions.

3.2.1. Status of the Plan

A variety of indicators will suggest if the plan is intended to be taken seriously. An obvious indication will be the level of commitment by participants to the planning process itself. An equally evident indicator is if the funds for implementing the plan are adequate. A clear sign of commitment on the part of government to the plan will be the enabling legislation that the plan may receive. A disaster preparedness plan has to be underwritten by the laws of the nation. Unless roles and responsibilities of ministries and individuals are reinforced by legal sanctions, implementation will be jeopardised. Whether that plan is a contingency plan focusing on specific types of emergencies or on specific geographic areas, or a national disaster preparedness strategy, there are certain features common to all such endeavors. Generally speaking, all planning exercises will have to address various points, which will eventually be incorporated into a planning document.

3.2.2. Institutional Structure

A coordinated disaster preparedness and response system is an essential condition of any disaster preparedness plan. There is no standard way of ensuring effective coordination. Each design will depend upon the traditions and governmental structure of the country under review. However, a plan will rapidly deteriorate unless there is "horizontal coordination" at central government and sub-national levels among ministries and specialized agencies and "vertical coordination" between central and local authorities. Avoid creating new organisations for disaster preparedness. Instead, work within established structures and systems. The emphasis must be upon strengthening existing institutions rather that devising additional layers of bureaucracy.

Disaster responses generally need the sanction of senior levels of government. For most disaster plans in the developing world, the approval of a president, prime minister or at least a deputy prime minister becomes the trigger mechanism for implementing a response. Consider the relationship between the senior level of government, ministerial levels and the functional disaster preparedness focal point.

An effective disaster preparedness plan will reflect an inter-ministerial response to disaster warnings and occurrences. These inter-ministerial committees, such as exist in India, should not be below the level of Permanent Secretary. This sort of committee will include a representative from the designated disaster preparedness focal point, and will keep appropriate senior government officials apprised on broad issues concerning preparedness and relief implementation. A focal point should be designated to ensure effective disaster preparedness and to act as a coordination mechanism for disaster response. This focal point can be attached to or become a specialised agency, such as a Relief and Rehabilitation Commission. A focal point can also be developed within a ministry regarded as essential for certain types of disasters.

A variety of institutional options related to regional and community structures also exist. In the Ethiopian National Disaster Prevention and Preparedness Strategy, the government has decided to have parallel systems at regional and local levels. Representatives from relevant central government ministries are located at regional and local levels to work hand in hand with committees comprised of representatives from local peasant associations, as well as local and regional officials. In China and India, however, regional and state governments respectively determine most of the functional activities needed to develop preparedness activities and to implement plans. Defining roles and responsibilities is one of the principal purposes of the plan. There is no standard method of delegation that will fit the requirements of all countries. There are, however, three points to keep in mind.

3.2.3. Roles and Responsibilities

Effective planners avoid imposing roles and responsibilities upon individuals or institutions that will not be capable of implementing them in the foreseeable future. Nor does it make sense to assign roles and responsibilities without regard to the political and social conditions of the country or relevant regions within the country. This is especially important regarding the functions of local officials and local institutions. Botawana's successful preparedness is due in part to the way it uses local tribal leaders to elicit information about needs instead of relying on a central government official who may be less familiar with particular areas and local relief requirements.

Assessing vulnerability builds a framework for on-going information updates about the infrastructure and socioeconomic conditions of disasterprone areas and vulnerable people. At a very early stag in the planning process, you should decide on who will be responsible for providing updates of vulnerability profiles and on the frequency of such exercises.

3.2.4. Information Systems

Early warning systems are normally comprised of various elements. They can stem in part from information provided by meteorological offices, by a Ministry of Health. One major criterion for an effective plan is an established system to ensure the coordination of all these different inputs.

An interministerial information committee can serve this purpose. This sort of committee has to have clear-cut guidelines, reporting formats and mechanisms as well as established reporting procedures. It is essential to link the disaster preparedness focal point to this committee. Perhaps the focal point might serve as the chair organisation for this interministerial information committee. An added complication involves the combination of this information with grass-roots information, the "early warning" information obtained from those most directly threatened, which is highly relevant and often ignored. Ensuring that appropriate information systems are in readiness includes stimulating information exchange systems within each agency in the emergency environment, between organisations and between the organisations and the public.

The most appropriate means of gathering and disseminating early warning information must be carefully assessed and well defined within the disaster preparedness plan. It is imperative that early warning messages be understood by the people for whom they are issued. Vulnerability assessment updates and the coordinated approach to early warning should encompass all the standard features required of any monitoring system. This includes determining changes in patterns of disaster threats, numbers of vulnerable people, and preparations for response. Monitoring must include an overall disaster preparedness assessment process in which essential physical aspects of the plan are reviewed system-wide to ensure that when disaster strikes, all that the plan anticipates is in place. Monitoring must also include an assessment process after a disaster strikes. This is meant to ensure that the implementation of the plan is efficient, and that appropriate and timely relief is being distributed to targeted beneficiaries. Specialised studies, such as transport capacity studies, will enhance the type of information and issues that should be built into early warning systems, vulnerability assessments and evaluations of resources required to implement the disaster preparedness plan.

The requirements to meet disaster needs will depend upon the types of disasters the plan anticipates. Such needs should be made explicit, and should cover all aspects of disaster relief and recovery implementation. Specific arrangements should be established whereby each party to written agreements can secure goods and services as required. Critical issues include special internal arrangements for the acquisition and dispersement of funds; policies and agreements for the use of other's equipment and services; and emergency funding strategies. In assessing the resources required for a disaster preparedness plan, the following elements should be considered.

3.2.5. Disaster Relief Funding

It is important to establish an emergency contingency fund. There is often a need for items that cannot be easily stockpiled, such as medicines, or items that were not anticipated, such as alternative fuels. A special reserve fund is worth considering in your preparedness plan.

Insurance is another form of creating reserves against potential future disasters. The following box illustrates one application of insurance.

3.2.6. Disaster Preparedness Funding

Solicit funds to pursue the activities of the planning process, including special studies, public awareness and training. Also seek funds to develop major inputs for the plan to function effectively.

3.2.7. Mechanism for Aid Coordination

Establish a means to ensure a coordinated, useful and timely response from the international community if and when its assistance is required. Not only should such a mechanism incorporate inputs from bilateral donors, but possible assistance from non-governmental organisations should also be brought into the coordinating mechanism.

3.2.8. Stockpiling

Consider the types and amounts of materials needed; whether they can be stockpiled, and where. This is not an easy task. In particularly disaster-prone countries, the very poverty that makes large segments of a society vulnerable to disasters means that stockpiling significant amounts of relief materials is a luxury. However, donors often are willing to make contributions to various forms of "stockpiling," such as food security reserves.

3.2.9. Public Education and Training

One emphasis of a disaster preparedness plan should be to anticipate the requirements for a disaster relief operation and the most effective ways of meeting those requirements. The planning process will only be effective if those who are the ultimate beneficiaries know what to do in times of disasters and know what to expect. For this reason, an essential part of a disaster preparedness plan is the education of those who may be threatened by disaster. Such education may take the following forms.

3.2.10. Public Education in Schools

Standardised curricula for children and young adults should include information about actions, which should be taken in case of a disaster threat or occurrence.

3.2.10.1. Special training courses

Workshops should be designed for an adult population, either specifically or as an extra dimension of on-going programs, such as literacy or cooperative training sites.

3.2.10.2. Extension programmes

Community of village-based outreach workers should be trained to provide relevant information.

3.2.10.3. Public information

Although television, radio and the printed media will never replace the impact of direct instruction, sensitively designed and projected messages can provide a useful supplement to the overall process. In establishing educational training, remember that education is often a two-way process in the field of disaster preparedness. For example, if a group does not fully comprehend the warning sequences in a tropical storm preparedness plan, it may be that the warning equences need to be reworked. Training of those who will implement portions of the disaster preparedness plan is essential. Those responsible for issuing warnings must be trained as well as those who will have direct relief functions. Training cannot be a one-time event. Refresher courses are essential. Training should be active in every way possible. Actual exercises should be performed, such as evacuation drills.

3.2.11. International Collaboration

Disaster preparedness plans and their implementation are the responsibility of the government. The United Nations can facilitate and enhance government efforts, but the government must formally initiate and control the disaster preparedness and response processes. In spite of government primacy in the realm of disaster preparedness, most emergency situations of significant magnitude in the developing world require some form of collaborative assistance from the international community. This part of the module focuses on ways the international community can support national government disaster preparedness activities. It also analyses how the United Nations system can facilitate these activities.

The terms "international community" and "international system" are largely abstractions. There are few manifestations of community or system when dealing with the various nations, international governmental and nongovernmental organisations that inhabit the globe. When discussing aspects of international involvement in disaster management, you will usually be dealing with a random assortment of governmental, non-governmental and international institutions that form part of an ad hoc network. This perspective of the international community includes three obstacles that directly affect disaster preparedness at the country level. The first is that support for national disaster preparedness efforts by those who might be most able to assist, such as bilateral donors, is by no means a certainty. Their assistance is not guaranteed. Therefore, it is important from the outset to establish the type of support a government's disaster preparedness initiative might receive. This will entail not only establishing an effective means of interesting such donors in these activities, but also effective means to keep them interested.

Secondly, there are many reasons why governments are wary of including "outsiders" in the formulation of a disaster strategy or plan.

3.3. Conclusion

When introducing disaster preparedness strategies or plans to government officials it is important to sensitise officials to the virtues of disaster preparedness: that an effective disaster preparedness plan will protect development, introduce disaster mitigation, strengthen local infrastructures and exert pressure on traditional aid donors. It is important to establish a reliable information base in order to prepare an effective disaster preparedness plan. The following information systems are highly recommended:

- vulnerability assessments;
- joint information programmes; crosschecking mechanisms in order to sort out conflicting data that may emerge; and
- joint-assessment processes in order to reduce duplication of efforts, promote a degree of consensus about damage and needs, and ensure joint endorsement of any aid appeals.

It is also essential to define appropriate institutional structures that will be responsible for plan design, rehearsal, implementation and evaluation. The roles and functions of responsible officials must be identified. Plans to coordinate the efforts of all designated ministries and procedures to include NGOs are needed. Mechanisms to determine the amount and type of assistance to be provided should be established. It is important that regional and local involvement be incorporated into the disaster preparedness planning process at all stages. This requires variations and flexibility in planning strategies in order to meet the specific conditions of particular areas.

References

Bohem, Hilda. Disaster Prevention and Disaster Preparedness . Berkeley: University of California, 1978.

Bulgawicz, Susan L. and Charles E. Nolan. Disaster Prevention and Recovery: A Planned Approach, Prairie Village: ARMA International, 1988.

Comfort, Louise K., ed. *Managing Disaster: Strategies and Policy Perspectives*, Durham: Duke University Press, 1988.

Genovese, Robert, Trish Taylor and Edward White, *Disaster Preparedness Manual*, Buffalo, N.Y. : W.S. Hein, 1989.

Mathieson, David, "Hurricane Preparedness: Establishing Workable Policies for Dealing with Storm Threats", *Technology and Conservation,* Summer 1983.

CHAPTER 2

Disaster Mitigation

4.1. Introduction

Disaster mitigation is the term used to refer to all actions to reduce the impact of a disaster that can be taken prior to its occurrence, including preparedness and long-term risk reduction measures. It includes both the planning and implementation of measures to reduce the risks associated with known natural and human-made hazards, and the process of planning for effective response to disasters, which do occur.

Mitigation is one of the positive links between disasters and development. Agencies, communities, and individuals can use their development resources to reduce the risk of hazards through mitigation projects. They can also ensure that their other development initiatives contain components that mitigate against future disaster. In its broadest usage, mitigation has become a collective term used to encompass all actions taken prior to the occurrence of a disaster (pre-disaster measures). This includes long-term risk reduction and preparedness measures.

Many individuals and institutions, however, apply a narrower definition to mitigation. They use mitigation to mean actions taken to reduce both human suffering and property loss resulting from extreme natural phenomena. The concept of mitigation accepts the fact that some hazard event may occur but tries to lessen the impact by improving the community's ability to absorb the impact with minimum damage or disruptive effect. More simply stated, for this group, mitigation is risk reduction.

Disaster have, until recently, been seen in much the same way as disease was in the early 19th century: unpredictable, unlucky and part of the everyday risk of living. Concentrations of people and rising population levels across the globe are increasing the risk of disasters and multiplying the consequences of natural hazards when they occur. However, the "epidemiology" of disasters-the systematic science of what happens in a disaster-shows that disasters are largely preventable. There are many ways to reduce the impact of a disaster and to mitigate the effects of a possible hazard, accident, or conflict. Just like the fight against disease, the fight against disasters has to be fought by everyone together. It must involve public and private sector investment, changes in social attitudes and improvements in the practices of individuals.

Governments can use public investment to improve their countries' infrastructure and to promote a physical environment where a disaster is less likely to occur. Individuals must also learn how to act to protect themselves. Just as public health depends on personal hygiene, so public protection depends on personal safety.

The type of cooking stove an individual uses, and their awareness that a sudden earthquake could tip it over is more important in reducing the risk of a disastrous fire than having the community maintain a large fire brigade. The type of house individuals build and where they consider a suitable place to live affects the potential for disaster in a community more than large engineering projects to reduce flood risk, or landslide stabilisation efforts or sophisticated typhoon warning systems.

The worst effects of any disaster are the deaths and injuries caused to the population. The scale of disasters and the number of people they are capable of killing is the primary justification for mitigation. Understanding the way that people are killed and injured in disasters is a prerequisite for reducing casualties.

4.2. Institutionalisation of Disaster Mitigation

Disaster mitigation also requires certain organisational and procedural measures. The time scale over which a significant reduction can be achieved in the potential impact of a disaster is medium and long term. Changes in location planning, upgrading structures and changes in the characteristics of building stock are process that take decades. The objectives and policies that guide the mitigation processes have to be sustained over a number of years. They have to survive the changes in political administration that are likely to happen within that time, the changes in budgetary priorities and policies on other matters. The institutionalisation of disaster mitigation means the acceptance of a consensus of opinion that efforts to reduce disaster risk are of continual importance. Education, training and the development of professional expertise are necessary components of institutionalising disaster mitigation.

4.2.1. Societal

The mitigation of disasters will only come about when there is a consensus that it is desirable. In many places, the individual hazards that threaten do not result in disasters, the steps that people can take to protect themselves are not known and the mandate of the community to have itself protected is not forthcoming. Mitigation planning should aim to develop a disaster "safety culture," one in which the general public is fully aware of potential hazards, chooses to protect itself as fully as possible and can readily support protective efforts made on its behalf.

4.2.2. Conflict Reduction

In the disasters and emergencies created by conflict, mitigation must include conflict reduction. Measures at conflict reduction must start with identifying and addressing the root causes of the conflict. Although negotiation will often be the primary tool of conflict reduction, the issues may arise over such causes as land tenure, employment, access to resources, and intolerance of ethnic or religious differences. These issues need to be anticipated through a form of early warning and defused before conflict erupts.

4.2.3. Timing for Mitigation

The risk reduction measures of mitigation are often placed in the pre-disaster time frame. In fact, the most opportune time to implement mitigation is in the period after a disaster. Public awareness of the problems posed by hazards is high and the political will to act may also be at its peak. This period probably will not last for more than two to three years before other development priorities take precedence.

4.3. Implementation of Disaster Mitigation Techniques

Mitigation means taking actions to reduce the effects of a hazard before it occurs. The term mitigation applies to a wide range of activities and protection measures that might be instigated, from the physical, like constructing stronger buildings, to the procedural, like standard techniques for incorporating hazard assessment in land-use planning. The 1990s will be a decade of major effort to encourage the implementation of disaster mitigation techniques in development projects around the world. The aim is to achieve a significant reduction in the loss of life and material damage caused by disasters by the end of the decade. DHA and UNDP will play a central role in encouraging national governments and non-governmental agencies to tackle disaster related issues through projects focused directly on reducing the impacts of hazards and through incorporation of risk awareness as part of the normal operations of development projects.

A useful analogy with the recently developing science of disaster mitigation is the implementation of public health measures that began in the mid 19th century. Before that time tuberculosis, typhoid, cholera, dysentery, smallpox and many other diseases were major causes of death and tended to assume epidemic proportions as the industrial development of cities fuelled increasing concentrations of population. These diseases had a major effect on life expectancy at the time and yet were regarded as just part of the everyday risks of living.

The apparent randomness with which the diseases struck and the unpredictability of epidemics meant that superstition, mythology and a certain amount of fatalism was the only public response to the hazards: the high risk of disease was generally accepted because there was little alternative. As the understanding of what caused diseases increased, chiefly through the efforts of scientists and epidemiologists in the 19th century, so the incidence of epidemics and illnesses generally became demystified.

It became evident that disease was preventable and gradually the concept of public protection against disease became accepted. It became evident that sanitation, purification of the water supply, garbage disposal and public hygiene were key issues for public health. The measures necessary to reduce the risk of disease were expensive-massive investment in infrastructure was needed to build sewers and clean water supply networks-and required major changes in public practices and attitudes. Social historians refer to this as the "Sanitary Revolution". Garbage collection and disposal had to be organised. It became socially unacceptable to throw garbage or to dispose of sewage in the streets.

Personal hygiene, washing and individual sanitation practices became important. Initially encouraged by public awareness campaigns, they gradually became part of the social norms and were taught by parents to their children. Attitudes changed from the previous fatalism about disease to a public health "safety culture", where everyone participated in reducing the risk of communal disease. Public health advances went hand-in-hand with public medicine, medical care, vaccination, preventive health care and a health industry that in most developed countries today consumes a very significant proportion of national economic production.

Today public epidemics are unacceptable. High levels of risk from disease are not tolerated and outbreaks of disease are followed by outbursts of public opinion demanding medical and government response to protect them. Everyone now considers it normal to participate in their own protection against health hazards and accepts the high levels of cost involved in society's battle against disease. The level of risk from public health hazards that is judged acceptable by modern society is far lower than it was three or four generations ago.

Disasters today are seen in much the same way as disease was in the early 19th century: unpredictable, unlucky and part of the everyday risk of living. Concentrations of people and rising population levels across the globe are increasing the risk of disasters and multiplying the consequences of natural hazards when they occur. However, the "epidemiology" of disasters-the systematic science of what happens in a disaster-shows that disasters are largely preventable. There are many ways to reduce the impact of a disaster and to mitigate the effects of a possible hazard or accident. Just like the fight against disease, the fight against disasters has to be fought by everyone together and involves public and private sector investment, changes in social attitudes and improvements in the practices of individuals. Just as the Sanitary Revolution occurred with the development of a "safety culture" for public health, so disaster mitigation has to develop through the evolution of an equivalent "safety culture" for public safety. Governments can use public investment to make stronger infrastructure and a physical environment where a disaster is less likely to occur, but individuals also have to act to protect themselves. Just as public health depends on personal hygiene, so public protection depends on personal safety.

The type of cooking stove an individual uses, and an awareness that a sudden earthquake could tip it over is more important in reducing the risk of conflagration than the community maintaining a large fire brigade. The type of house an individual builds and the sites that each individual considers a suitable place to live affects the potential for disaster in a community more than large engineering projects to reduce flood risk or landslide stabilisation or sophisticated typhoon warning systems.

The science of disasters is in a similar state of development to that of epidemiology in the latter half of the 19th century: the causes, mechanisms and processes of disasters are becoming understood rapidly. As a result of this understanding, the more developed countries have begun to implement individual measures to reduce the risk of future disasters. A catalogue of techniques are known for disaster mitigation, and their relevance to the countries that need them most is now clear. Disasters are very largely a developmental issue. The great majority of casualties and disaster effects are suffered in developing countries. Development achievements can be wiped out by a major disaster and economic growth reversed. The promotion of disaster mitigation in the projects and planning activities of development protects development achievement and assists populations in protecting themselves against needless injury.

4.3.1. Effects of Hazards

The most critical part of implementing mitigation is the full understanding of the nature of the threat. In each country and in each region, the types of hazards faced are different. Some countries are prone to floods, others have histories of tropical storm damage, and others are known to be in earthquake regions. Most countries are prone to some combination of the various hazards and all face the possibility of technological disasters as industrial development progresses. The effects these hazards are likely to have and the damage they are likely to cause depends on what is present in the region: the people, their houses, sources of livelihood and infrastructure. Each country is different. For any particular location or country it is critical to know the types of hazards likely to be encountered.

The understanding of natural hazards and the processes that cause them is the province of seismologists, volcanologists, climatologists, hydrologists and other scientists. The effects of natural hazards on structures and the man-made environment is the subject of studies by engineers and risk specialists. Death and injury caused by disasters and the consequences of damage in terms of the disruption to society and its impact on the economy is a research area for medical practitioners, economists and social scientists. The science is still relatively young-most of the recordings of damaging earthquakes by strong motion instruments were obtained in the past twenty years, for example, and only since satellite photography has it been possible to routinely track tropical storms. The understanding of the consequences of failure of social organisations and regional economies is even more recent.

The worst effects of any disaster are the deaths and injuries caused. The scale of disasters and the number of people they kill are the primary justifications for mitigation. Understanding the way that people are killed and injured in disasters is a prerequisite for reducing casualties. Among the sudden onset disasters, floods and earthquakes cause the most casualties worldwide, with storms and high winds being less deadly but far more widespread. The consequences of physical damage are often more important than the damage itself. A damaged factory can no longer continue to jobs. The jobless have no income to spend in their local shops and the whole local economy suffers. Damage to infrastructure and to the means of production depresses the economy.

Mitigation also entails the protection of the economy from disasters. Economic activity in the more industrialised societies is complex and interdependent, with service industries dependent on manufacturing, which in turn relies on supplies of raw materials, labour, power and communications. This complex interdependency is extremely vulnerable to disruption by hazards affecting any one link in the chain. Newly industrialising societies are most vulnerable of all.

Agricultural sectors of the economy are most vulnerable to drought but also to floods and high winds, disease and pest attack and pollution. Industry is more vulnerable to earthquake damage and the disruption of transportation and utilities networks. Commerce and finance are most vulnerable to disruption of production, population migration and to breakdowns in communications systems. Mitigation measures that focus on protecting the most vulnerable elements and activities-the weakest links-in the different sectors of the economy will help protect the achievements of economic development.

4.3.2. Targeting Mitigation

The understanding of how the occurrence of a natural hazard or an accident turns into a disaster enables us to forecast likely situations where disasters are possible. If there were no human settlements or economic activities affected, an earthquake would be a harmless act of nature. The combination of settlements (elements) and earthquake (hazard) makes the disaster possible.

Disasters are often the result of combinations of factors occurring together: a fire source, a dense residential area and combustible houses for example, or a seismic fault rupturing close to a city formed of high occupancy weak buildings. The contributory factors of past disasters can be identified to highlight similar conditions elsewhere. This is the process of risk analysis.

Identifying situations where combinations of risk factors coincide indicates the elements most at risk. The elements most at risk are the buildings, community services, infrastructure and activities that will suffer most from the effects of the hazard or will be least able to recover after the event. At a regional level, the concentrations of population and infrastructure in large cities make it likely that the losses inflicted by even low levels of hazard will exceed the total losses inflicted by severe levels of hazard on all the villages in the region. Mitigation measures in the city may have the most effect in reducing future losses. The portions of the housing stock in the city most likely to be damaged can be identified and mitigation measures applied to that sector will have the effect on reducing risk. The number of elements likely to be affected by a hazard, together with their vulnerability to the hazard will identify where mitigation is most effective.

4.3.3. Vulnerability

Houses built form cane and thatch that can be blown apart in a tropical storm are more vulnerable to wind loads than a brick building. A brick building is more likely to disintegrate with the violent ground shaking of an earthquake than a strong reinforced concrete frame structure (or cane and thatch hut) and is more vulnerable to earthquake hazard. Vulnerability is the degree of expected damage form a particular hazard. Targeting mitigation efforts relies heavily on correctly assessing vulnerability.

This concept of vulnerability assessment can also be extended to social groups or economic sectors: People who rent their houses rely on a landlord to repair the damage and are more likely to be made homeless in the event of a disaster. Correctly identifying the groups of tenants and establishing rights of tenure and landlords' obligations to repair may reduce the number of people made homeless in a disaster. Similarly, food growers sending their produce to market through a single mountain pass will be unable to sell their produce if the pass is blocked. Developing an alternative route to market will reduce the vulnerability of the agricultural sector to damage by disaster.

4.4. Reducing Hazard and Vulnerability

Protection against threats can be achieved by removing the causes of the threat, (reducing the hazard) or by reducing the effects of the threat if it occurs (reducing the vulnerability of elements at risk). For most types of natural disaster, it is impossible to prevent the actual geological or meteorological process from occurring: volcanos erupt, earthquakes occur, cyclones and wind storms rage. The focus of mitigation policies against these hazards is primarily on reducing the vulnerability of elements that are likely to be affected. Some natural hazards can be reduced in certain circumstances.

The construction of levees along the banks of certain rivers reduces the chance of them flooding the surrounding areas, for example, and it is possible to prevent known landslides and rockfalls from developing further by stabilising land pressures, constructing retaining walls and improving drainage of slopes. The destructive agents of some natural hazards can be contained by engineering works or diverted away from important elements in channels and excavations. In some cases tree planting can be an effective way of either reducing the potential for floods and mudslides or to slow desertification. The potential for reducing the hazard level is given in each of the hazard profiles.

Obviously, preventing industrial accidents from occurring in the first place is the best method of mitigating future industrial disasters. Fire prevention, chemical spillage, technological and transportation accidents are all hazards that are essentially preventable. In man-made risks of disaster the focus of disaster mitigation is in reducing or preventing the hazards from occurring. Engineering system safety is an important part of reducing risks form industrial hazards. A growing body of knowledge form the experience of long-established industries is applicable to the newly-industrialising regions.

4.4.1. Tools, Powers and Budgets

From the hazard profiles and the descriptions of actions that may be possible to reduce their effects, it is evident that protection is complex and needs to be built up through a range of activities undertaken at the same time. Protection cannot be simply provided by any single authority or agency. A government cannot provide housing that is wind-resistant for every citizen in cycloneprone areas. Governments can and do, however, influence individuals towards protecting themselves and the rest of the community. Governments can employ a wide range of tools and use their powers in many ways to influence the safety of the community. Legislative powers, administrative functions, spending and project initiation are all tools they can employ to bring about change.

Safety standards, construction codes and building regulations form part of the normal apparatus that government use to help a community protect itself. One of the simplest measures for national authorities to take is to pass legislation for a national building code that requires new buildings and infrastructures to be resistant to the various hazard prevalent in that country. Some 40 earthquake-prone countries currently have seismic building codes for new construction. However, codes themselves are likely to have little effect unless the building designers are aware of them and understand them, and unless the community considers them necessary, and unless they are enforced by competent administrators.

The multiplicity of hazards and the different ways of reducing their various effects on the elements at risk is further compounded by the type of community powers and budgets available to the decision-makers. There is no standard solution to mitigating a disaster risk. The construction of large scale engineering projects in Japan and other high-income countries to give protection against floods and volcanic debris flows, is not appropriate to mitigating similar hazards in developing countries. The enforcement of town planning regulations, and what is considered an acceptable level of interference by an authority on individual's right to build, varies considerably from one country to another, it varies from rural to urban situations and from one community and culture to the next.

4.5. Community-based Mitigation

It has been argued that governments and large development agencies tend to adopt a "top-down" approach to disaster mitigation planning whereby the intended beneficiaries are provided with solutions designed for them by planners rather than selected for themselves. Such "top-down" approaches tend to emphasise physical mitigation measures rather than social changes to build up the resources of the vulnerable groups. They rarely achieve their goals because they act on symptoms not causes, and fail to respond to the real needs and demands of the people. Ultimately they undermine the community's own ability to protect itself.

An alternative approach is to develop mitigation policies in consultation with local community groups using techniques and actions, which they can organise themselves and manage with limited outside technical assistance. Such community-based mitigation programs are considered more likely to result in actions which are a response to people's real needs, and to contribute to the development of the community, its consciousness of the hazards it faces and its ability to protect itself in the future, even though technically the means may be less effective than larger-scale mitigation programmes. They will also tend to maximise the use of local resources, including labour, materials and organisation. Applying such community-based policies depends on several factors-the existence of active concerned local community groups and agencies able to provide technical assistance and support at an appropriate level, for example, are crucial to success.

Nevertheless, opportunities for community-based mitigation actions should always be sought in developing a comprehensive mitigation strategy. They will certainly be cheaper and may be more successful than alternative larger-scale programmes.

4.5.1. Engineering and Construction Measures

Engineering measures are of two types. Those that result in stronger individual structures that are more resistant to hazards, and those that create structures whose function is primarily disaster protection-flood control structures, dikes, levees, infiltration dams, etc. Actions of the first type are mainly actions on individual buildings and structures and are sometimes referred to as "hardening" facilities against hazard forces. Improving the design and construction of buildings, agricultural structures, infrastructure and other facilities can be achieved in a number of ways.

Design standards, building codes and performance specifications are important for facilities designed by engineers. Engineering design against the various hazards may include design for vibration, lateral loads, load surcharges, wind loads, impact, combustibility, flood resistance and other safety factors. Building codes are the critical front line defense for achieving stronger engineered structures, including large private buildings, public sector buildings, infrastructure, transportation networks and industrial facilities.

Disaster-resistance based building codes are unlikely to result in stronger buildings unless the engineers who have to implement the code accept its importance and endorse its use, understand the code and the design criteria required of them and unless the code is fully enforced by authorities through checking and penalising designs that do not comply. A code has to fit into an environment prepared to receive it. Part of the measures necessary to achieve the "engineering" mitigation measures may include increased levels of training for engineers and designers, explanatory manuals to interpret the code requirements and the establishment of an effective administration to check code compliance in practice: the recruitment of ten new municipal engineers to enforce an existing code may have more effect in increasing construction quality in a city than proposing higher standards in building codes.

A large number of the buildings likely to be affected in a disaster, and those most vulnerable to hazards are not designed by engineers and will be unaffected by safety standards established in the building codes. These are houses, workshops, storerooms and agricultural buildings built by the owners themselves or by craftsmen or building contractors to their own designs. In many countries these non-engineered buildings make up a large percentage of the total building stock. The "engineering" measures that are needed to improve the disaster-resistance of non-engineered structures involve the education of builders in practical construction techniques. The resistance of houses to cyclone winds is ultimately dependent on how well the roofing sheets are nailed down, and the quality of the joints in the building frame and its attachment to the ground. Training techniques to teach builders the practicalities of disaster resistant construction are now well understood and form part of the menu of mitigation actions available to the disaster manager.

Persuading owners and communities to build safer, more disaster resistant structures and to pay the additional costs involved is required to make builder training effective. The building contractor may play a role in persuading the client to build to higher specifications, but unless this is carried out within a general public awareness of the disaster risk and acceptance of the need for protection, the contractor is unlikely to find many customers. Grant systems, preferential loans and supply of building materials have also been used as incentives to help improve the hazard resistance of non-engineered buildings. Legalising land ownership and giving tenants protective rights also encourages people to upgrade building stock with security of tenure and a stake in their own future. Apart form new buildings, the existing building stock also may need to be "hardened" against future hazard impacts.

The cost of adding strength to an existing building tends to be more expensive (and disruptive) than making new building design stronger, so strengthening is unlikely to be an economic option for the large majority of the building stock; for average buildings, with relatively short life expectancies, it may be better to take a long-term view of building stock upgrading, waiting until buildings come naturally to the end of their useful lives, demolishing them and buildings new structures in their place that conform to building code safety requirements. For special structures, critical facilities or historic buildings with long expected life spans, retrofit strengthening techniques are now well established and a considerable amount of expertise has been developed in this field, though these are generally too costly to be useful in development projects. The engineering of large-scale flood control and water-supply measures is complex, lengthy and capital-intensive; and their construction frequently has adverse consequences for those they are intended to protect, for example some people may be forced off their land, land-use patterns may be changed and other adverse effects felt. Experience has shown that small-scale flood control measures which can be managed by community-based organisations can be effective in risk mitigation while simultaneously achieving other development goals. They tend to make use of local materials, labour and management resources to build on traditional mitigation knowledge rather than replacing it, and to enhance the community's own self-reliance rather than undermining it. Such measures can play an important role in disaster mitigation within integrated agricultural or rural development projects.

4.5.2. Physical Planning Measures

Many hazards are localised with their likely effects confined to specific known areas: Floods affect flood plains, landslides affect steep soft slopes, etc. The effects can be greatly reduced if it is possible to avoid the hazardous areas being used for settlements or as sites for important structures. Most urban masterplans involving land use zoning probably already attempt to separate hazardous industrial activities from major population centers. Urban planning needs to integrate awareness of natural hazards and disaster risk mitigation into the normal processes of planning the development of a city. Location of public sector facilities is easier to control than private sector location or land use. The careful location of public sector facilities can itself play an important role in reducing the vulnerability of a settlement-schools, hospitals, emergency facilities and major infrastructural elements like water pumping stations, electrical power transformers and telephone exchanges represent a significant proportion of the functioning of a town. An important principle is deconcentration of elements at risk: services provided by one central facility are always more at risk than those provided by several smaller facilities. The collapse of the central telephone exchange in the Mexico City earthquake of 1985 cut communications in the city completely. In the reconstruction, the central exchange was replaced by a number of mini exchanges in different locations around the city to make the telephone system less vulnerable. The same principle applies equally to hospitals and schools, for example as it does to power stations and water treatment plants.

The principle of deconcentration also applies to population densities in a city: a denser concentration of people will always have more disaster potential than if they are more dispersed. Where building densities can be controlled the urban masterplan should reflect the spatial distribution of hazard severity levels in its zoning for permitted densities of development. Indirect control of densities is sometimes possible through simpler methods such as using wide roads, height limitations and road layouts that limit the size of plots available for development. Creation of park lands reduces urban densities, and also provides space in the city, greenery, allows drainage to decrease flood risk, provides refuge areas for the population in the event of urban fires and may provide space for emergency facilities in the event of a disaster.

At a regional level, the concentration of population growth and industrial development in a centralised city is generally less desirable than a decentralised pattern of secondary towns, satellite centers and development spread over a broader region.

The design of service networks-roads, pipelines, and cables also needs careful planning to reduce risk of failure. Long lengths of supply line are at risk if they are cut at any point. Networks that interconnect and allow more than one route to any point are less vulnerable to local failures provided that individual sections can be isolated when necessary. Vehicle access to a specific point is less likely to be cut by a road blockage in a circular road system than in a radial one.

Urban planners may also be able to reduce risks by changing the use of a vulnerable building being used for an important function-a school in a weak building could be moved to a stronger building and the weak building used for a less important function, like storage.

The location of public sector facilities is easier to control than those in the private sector. In many rapidly developing cities, the control of private sector land use through urban masterplanning and development permissions is almost impossible. It is often private sector land use, the informal sectors and shantytowns that pose the highest risks of disaster. Flood plains and steep slopes are often the marginal lands that are available to the lower-income communities and the most vulnerable social groups. The economic pressures that drive these groups, first to the city for jobs and opportunity, and second to the marginal lands to live, need to be fully understood as the context for reducing their risk. Prohibition or measures to clear settlers from hazardous areas are unlikely to be successful for long if the background pressures are not addressed. Some indirect measures may be effective, such as making safer land available, or making alternative locations more attractive. This may be through better provision of income sources, access to public transport and better service provision. Deterring further development in unoccupied areas by declaring areas clearly as hazard zones, denying services, reducing accessibility and limiting availability of building materials may also be effective. Ultimately, however, it is only when the local community recognises the true extent of the hazard and accepts that the risk outweighs the benefit to them of being in that location that they will locate elsewhere or protect themselves in other ways.

4.5.3. Economic Measures

Equitable economic development is the key to disaster mitigation. A strong economy in which the benefits are shared throughout the society is the best protection against a future disaster. A strong economy means more money to spend on stronger buildings and larger financial reserves to cope with future losses. The interdependency between Disasters and Development is the subject of another module in this training course. Mitigation measures that help the community reduce future economic losses, help members withstand losses and improve their ability to recover after loss and measures that make it possible for communities to afford higher levels of safety are important elements of an overall mitigation programme.

Inevitably it is those who have least that, proportionally, lose most in a disaster. The weakest members of the economy have few economic reserves. If they lose their house or their animals they have no means of recovering them. They are unlikely to have insurance or access to credit and can quickly become destitute. Large scale drought or flood disasters in rural areas can result in an acceleration of urbanisation in the region and possibly increased risks as families with their livelihoods destroyed migrate to the towns in search of better opportunities. The destruction of industries and loss of jobs and incomes may well make recovery of the region a long and slow process or make it more vulnerable to a future disaster. Reconstruction plans often extend generous loans to victims to aid their recovery but a family without an income has little prospect of making repayments and is therefore unable to benefit.

Economic development is likely to be the main objective of any regional planner or national government agency, regardless of disaster mitigation objectives. The processes of economic development are complex and beyond the direct focus of this training course, however, disaster mitigation should be seen as a part of the process of economic development. Some aspects of economic planning are directly relevant to reducing disaster risk. Diversification of economic activity is as important an economic principle as deconcentration is in physical planning. A single industry (or single-crop) economy is always more vulnerable than an economy made up of many different activities. The linkages between different sectors of an economy-the transportation of goods, the flow of information, the labour market-may be more vulnerable to disruption from a disaster than the physical infrastructure that is the means of production. Tourism as an economic sector is extremely vulnerable to disaster, or even the rumour of a potential disaster. The reliance of industry and the economy on infrastructure-the roads, transportation networks, power, telephone services etc., means that a high priority should be placed on protecting these facilities: the consequential losses of failure are costly to the whole community.

Economic incentives and penalties are an important part of the powers of any authority. Grants, loans, taxes, tax concessions and fines can be used to influence the decisions people make to reduce disaster-related risks. Industrial location is commonly influenced by government incentives which can be used to attract industry to safer locations or to act as a focus for and loans can be offered to assist owners to upgrade their property and make buildings more disaster resistant. In industrialised countries, insurance is one of the major economic protection devices. If the risk of economic loss is spread widely over a large number of premium payers, the loss is safely dissipated. Commercial insurance is expensive and its viability is determined by accurate calculation of risk. With only a small number of premium payers, premiums remain high and are prohibitive to potential policy holders. The more widespread policy holding becomes, the lower the premiums are and the more widespread insurance use is likely to be. Encouragement of people to protect themselves through insurance ensures that a level of protection is built up.

Compulsory insurance schemes have not been successful and national governments rarely have the financial resources to dedicate to disaster insurance guarantees, although many countries build up a disaster reconstruction fund through general taxation. Disaster insurance is high-risk finance and only multinational insurance companies can gather the resources to cover the losses of any sizeable disaster. It is unlikely to be available to protect poorer or rural communities and their disaster-protection investments unless backed by a large development agency.

4.5.4. Management and Institutional Measures

Disaster mitigation also requires certain organisational and procedural measures. The time span over which a significant reduction can be achieved in the potential for disaster is long. Changes in physical planning, upgranding structures and changes in the characteristics of building stock are processes that take decades. The objectives and policies that guide the mitigation processes have to be sustained over a number of years, and have to survive the changes in political administration that are likely to happen within that time, the changes in budgetary priorities and policies on other matters.

The institutionalisation of disaster mitigation requires a consensus of opinion that efforts to reduce disaster risk are of continual importance. Education, training and professional competence, and political will, are necessary aspects of institutionalising disaster mitigation. The professional training of engineers, planners, economists, social scientist and other managers to include hazards and risk reduction within their normal area of competence is gradually becoming common. Increasing the exposure of these groups to international expertise and transfer of technology in disaster mitigation is an important part of building capability in the affected country. Information is a critical element in planning for disaster mitigation, but there are many hazard-prone countries where the basic meteorological and geological observatories to monitor hazards have not been established or do not have the resources to carry out their job.

Administrative and organisational powers for disaster mitigation include the checking procedures and planning powers to realise mitigation plans, consultation procedures and representation of the community in mitigation decisions and management of the implementation of mitigation activities.

4.5.5. Societal Measures

The mitigation of disasters will only come about when there is a consensus that it is desirable, feasible and affordable. In many places, the individual hazards that threaten are not recognised, the steps that people can take to protect themselves are not known and the demand of the community to have themselves protected is not forthcoming. Mitigation planning should aim to develop a disaster "safety culture" in which the people are fully aware of the hazards they face, protect themselves as fully as they can and fully support efforts made on their behalf to protect them. Public awareness can be raised in a number of ways, from short-term, high-profile campaigns using broadcasts, literature and posters, to more long-term, low-profile campaigns that are carried out through general education.

Everyone who lives in a hazard-prone area should understand hazards as a fact of life. Information about hazards should be part of the standard curriculum of children at school and be part of everyday information sources, with occasional mentions of them in stories, TV soap operas, newspapers and other common media. The objective is to develop and everyday acknowledgment of hazard safety where people take conscious, automatic precautions through being aware of, but not terrified of, the possibility of hazard occurrence. Their understanding should include being aware of what to do in the event, and a sense that their choice of house, the placement of that bookcase or stove and the quality of construction of the garden wall around their children's area all affect their own safety.

The aim of a mitigation strategy is to reduce losses in the event of a future occurrence of a hazard. The primary aim is to reduce the risk of death and injury to the population. Secondary aims include reducing damage and economic losses inflicted on public sector infrastructure and reducing private sector losses in as far as they are likely to affect the community as whole. The objectives are likely to include encouragement for people to protect themselves as far as possible. A set of actions that includes some engineering measures, some spatial planning, and a degree of economic, management and societal inputs will be needed to bring about effective mitigation.

A mitigation programme that concentrates solely on any one of these five aspects will be unbalanced and is unlikely to achieve its aims. A mitigation strategy has to be designed for its proposed application. Disaster mitigation programs carried out in the Philippines are unlikely to be directly transferrable to Peru. There are few standard solutions. Some individual elements and techniques of mitigation will be transferrable compulsory purchase techniques for widening roads in dense urban areas that have been used in Peru may be of interest to the planners in the Philippines-but the full range of measures needed to reduce disaster potential for an individual application is likely to be unique. In each country the range of hazards faced are likely to be different.

4.6. Practicalities of Mitigation

Successful mitigation entails a number of fundamental changes in the attitudes of the people at risk, in the processes of creating and modifying the physical environment and in the physical layout of a community. These changes take time. The nature of political administrations requires that projects resulting in tangible or demonstrable outputs within the lifetime of the administration are preferred. Many visible elements of mitigation can be achieved within that time span; engineering projects for hazard mitigation, building strengthening, changing the use of vulnerable structures, widening streets, for example, but these alone are unlikely to result in a sustainable reduction in risk. A balance of immediately visible outputs and long term, sustainable benefits is needed. Financial incentive schemes to reduce disaster risk require a considerable government budget for disaster mitigation. The scale of the problem faced in trying to combat a large-scale hazard like earthquakes or tropical storms is the geographical extent of the zone at risk and the number of elements at risk in the region. Programs for housing upgrading, hazard education or community action is likely to involve millions of households. The resources necessary to accomplish this may be considerable.

4.6.1. Opportunities for Mitigation

Occasionally mitigation projects are prompted by predictions and studies of the likely consequences of hazards but in many cases implementation of mitigation comes about mainly in the aftermath of disaster. Rebuilding what has been destroyed and recognition that the damage was avoidable can generate protection against a future disaster. Public support for mitigation action is strong with the visible evidence and recent memory of the disaster, or the knowledge of a disaster elsewhere.

4.6.2. Community-based Mitigation

Successful mitigation practices must involve collaboration between the local community and largerscale development agencies. The local community must be aware of the risk and concerned to take action to prevent it: in this they may need technical assistance, material assistance and help in building their own capabilities. These forms of assistance may not be available in which case they need to be provided by external agencies. One of the most effective ways in which such an agency can help promote community protection is by enabling communities to formulate their own project proposals and negotiate with government and the larger development agencies (or government agencies) for the necessary government actions and the material assistance they need. This is especially true for technologically based engineering projects, such as large embankments, spillways, and diversion works.

References

Alexander, D., "The Study of Natural Disasters 1977-1997: Some Reflections on a Changing Field of Knowledge", *Disasters* 21 (4): 284-304, 1997.

Armenian, H. K., A. K. Melkonian, and A. P. Hovanesian, "Long-Term Mortality and Morbidity Related to Degree of Damage Following the Earthquake in Armenia", *American Journal of Epidemiology,* 1998.

Bernstein, R. S., P. J. Baxter, and A. S. Buist, "Introduction to the Epidemiological Aspects of Explosive Volcanism", *American Journal of Public Health,* 1986.

Buist, A. S., and R. S. Bernstein, "Health Effects of Volcanoes: An Approach to Evaluating the Health Effects of an Environmental Hazard", *American Journal of Public Health* 76 (Suppl.):1-2, 1986.

Chang, S. E., and C. Chamberlin, "Assessing the Role of Lifeline Systems in Community Disaster Resilience", *In Research Progress and Accomplishments 2003-2004, Multidisciplinary Center for Earthquake Engineering Research*, Buffalo, NY: 87-94, 2004.

Howard, M. J., J. C. Brillman, and F. M. Burkle, "Infectious Disease Emergencies in Disasters", *Emergency Medicine Clinics in North America* 14 (2): 413-28, 1996.

Malilay, J., M. G. Real, A. Ramirez Vanegas, E. Noji, and T. Sinks, "Public Health Surveillance after a Volcanic Eruption: Lessons from Cerro Negro, Nicaragua, 1992", *Bulletin of the Pan American Health Organization,* 1996.

Morgan, O., "Infectious Disease Risks from Dead Bodies Following Natural Disasters", *Revista Panamericana de Salud Publica,* 2004.

CHAPTER 5

Forecasting and Warning of Disasters

5.1. Warning

A warning is a risk communication about an imminent event and is intended to produce an appropriate disaster response. Examples of disaster responses include evacuating and sheltering in-place. There are eight stages of a person's information processing during a warning. However, before these stages begin, people must receive, heed, and comprehend information about the risks.

5.1.1. Step 1: Risk Identification

Decisions about how to respond to a hazard begin with risk identification. This process begins with the detection of environmental cues. However, the most important sources of risk identification are warning messages from authorities, the media, and peers. The first step you must take is to disseminate your message widely. Try to attract the attention of those at risk and inform them of the potential for disaster that threatens their health, safety and property.

5.1.2. Step 2: Risk Assessment

Risk assessment involves evaluating the personal consequences if the disaster occurs. People's personal risk assessment-their risk perception-is critical in understanding their disaster response. If people think they are in danger, then they are more likely to protect themselves. Peoples' risk assessments include the perceived probability, magnitude, and immediacy of the disaster impact. Perceived probability of impact affects people's judgments of the likelihood that they will be affected, whereas perceptions of event magnitude increase their perceptions of the severity of personal consequences, including death, injury, and property damage. As perceived probability and magnitude increase, so do a person's likelihood of taking protective action. The perceived immediacy of disaster impact affects people in a different way. Instead of affecting a person's likelihood of acting, perceived immediacy increases a person's urgency to act.

5.1.3. Step 3: Protective Action Search

The primary question in protective action search is "How can I protect myself?" Residents' first attempts to answer this question often involve a search for what can be done by someone else to protect them against the hazard. However, when disaster impact is imminent, household owners must rely mostly on their own resources to achieve protection. In many instances, an individual's knowledge of the hazard suggests what type of protection to seek.

People are likely to recall actions they have taken on previous occasions if they have had experience with that hazard. Alternatively, they might consider actions they took in similar hazards. For example, they might recognise that the impact of a volcanic mudflow is similar to that of a flood and, thus, they might take the protective responses that they took for a flood during a mudflow.

5.1.4. Step 4: Protective Action Assessment

Those at risk generally have at least two options-taking protective action or continuing normal activities. Sometimes, those at risk must choose between two alternatives, but they don't really like either of them. During a hurricane, for example, evacuation protects people, but abandons property to storm damage. On the other hand, emergency measures to protect property (e.g., sandbagging) require the property owner to remain in a hazardous location.

When no one option seems better than other options or continuing normal activities, it is difficult for people to decide what to do. For example, evacuation is a superior protective action than seeking shelter during a hurricane, but it also costs more in terms of money and time. For people on the fringes of an evacuation area, the risk of staying may be offset by the cost of evacuating. This can cause people to wait for further information about the hurricane to see if the risk has changed enough to push the balance more clearly one way or the other.

5.1.5. Step 5: Protective Action Implementation

Protective action implementation occurs when those at risk know they have to take action. People sometimes postpone taking action even when faced with danger. For example, some recipients of hurricane warnings often endanger their safety by waiting until the last minute to evacuate. Unfortunately, they fail to recognise that bad weather and a high traffic volume reduces the speed of evacuating vehicles. These conditions may lead to an incomplete evacuation before the arrival of storm conditions. The problem of procrastination is worse for long-term hazard adjustment without specific timetables.

5.1.6. Step 6: Information Needs Assessment

People who are taking protective action need information. Before taking action, they must decide if they have enough information. Any confusing messages or expressed doubts from officials will cause people to seek more information.

5.1.7. Step 7: Communication Action Assessment

Uncertainty about risk identification and risk assessment can stimulate questions directed to officials and, more likely, the news media. People often rely on the news media to confirm information they received about the hazard from other sources. However, people often consult their peers about what to do and how to do it. It is difficult for people to reach authorities because they are usually busy handling other calls. People are often forced to rely on the media and their peers even when they would prefer to contact authorities.

5.1.8. Step 8: Communication Action Implementation

The last question is, Do I need the information now? If the answer is yes, then people will seek the information. People will go to great lengths, contacting. For Example, after every hurricane, researchers find that some people failed to evacuate because they didn't believe the threat was likely to affect them. Part of this is due to the difficulty in predicting hurricanes. Sometimes forecasters predict that a strong hurricane will make landfall in one place but it turns and strikes somewhere else. This can lower people's perceived probability of a hurricane strike. Other times people expect the hurricane to strike but they don't expect it to affect them.

People will not work as hard to get information unless the threat is imminent. For example, many residents close to Mt. St. Helens checked radio news bulletins several times a day after the initial ash and steam eruptions led authorities to believe there was a high probability of a larger eruption. Without specific threat information, people tend to passively monitor the situation.

5.2. Risk Communication in Hazard Phase

The continuing hazard phase is marked by a low probability that a catastrophic incident will threaten public safety, property, and the environment. During this phase, people should engage in hazard mitigation, emergency preparedness, and recovery preparedness actions. In addition, they should also pursue an active programme of risk communication.

5.2.1. Step 1: Conduct a Strategic Analysis

The first step is to understand who is at risk. Then should understand the likelihood of different hazards. Knowing what types of hazards are threatening helps identify what actions people should take to protect themselves. Identifying the geographic areas at greatest risk makes it possible to identify the most vulnerable population segments and types of businesses. Knowing the vulnerable population segments and types of businesses provides information about how to communicate the risk. This information also helps you pick which incentives and sanctions will get people to adopt hazard adjustments.

5.2.1.1. Community's perception

The hazards that produce the greatest community conflict are those having a potential for inflicting significant harm on bystanders. These hazards include nuclear power plants and chemical facilities. People perceive these risks as greater than those of other technologies and other natural hazards.

Most people believe the risks of technological facilities are greater than those of natural hazards. And yet, the annual fatality rate is the same for both types of hazards. This problem can be addressed by explaining the concepts of risk analysis. However, one should recognise that it is difficult even for experts to understand small probabilities of occurrence such as one in a million. Some experts believe that if people accept risks having higher fatality rates, like driving, they also should accept risks having a lower fatality rate such as having a nuclear power plant nearby. This ignores the fact that the facility risk will be added to the lifestyle risk, not substituted for it. In addition, the facility risk is estimated from analytical models but the lifestyle risk is computed from a large database. Even local residents who cannot articulate these distinctions seem to be aware of them intuitively and reject risk analysis results.

5.2.1.2. Risk communication programme

Hazard awareness is an important first step in the process of hazard adjustment. People must be informed about the hazards to which their community is exposed and should be given this information from different perspectives. For example, people should know what a disaster would mean in terms of the public health. In addition, they need to know how likely it is that a disaster will occur where they live. In the case of hurricanes, a reasonable goal is to ensure residents understand the causes of hurricanes, the probabilities of being struck by a hurricane over the next ten years, and the threats hurricanes bring. Also, local residents should understand the risk to themselves and their families, damage to their property, and disruption to daily activities.

To help people understand, a risk communication programme should provide detailed maps showing areas at risk from wind, storm surge, and inland flooding. Explain the vulnerability of different buildings to these threats. Provide information about the personal consequences of hazard impact by showing drawings of different types of structures. Show mobile homes, typical single-family residences, and typical multifamily structures and the level of expected damage from each hurricane category. Develop this information carefully as recent studies found that only one- to two-thirds of coastal residents can accurately identify their hurricane risk areas.

5.2.2. Step 2: Perform an Operational Analysis

An emergency manager should perform five tasks when performing an operational analysis.

5.2.2.1. Task 1: Identify and assess feasible hazard adjustments for the community and its households/businesses

The purpose of this task is to make sure people know how to protect themselves. One can help people evaluate these in terms of resource requirements, such as financial cost, time and effort, knowledge and skill, tools and equipment, and required cooperation with others.

5.2.2.2. Task 2: Identify ways to provide incentives, sanctions, and technological innovations

To encourage people to protect themselves, one may have to punish them with sanctions, reward them with incentives, or inform them about technological innovations. Sanctions are appealing because they avoid the obvious costs associated with incentives. For example, ticketing drivers who don't wear seatbelts was a successful sanction. However, sanctions require enforcement. Your jurisdiction can reduce the costs of preparing for hazards by providing incentives such as grants, low interest rate loans, or tax credits. An alternative incentive, providing specific plans or checklists for hazard adjustments, is informational rather than financial. For example, providing plans for homeowners to bolt their houses to their foundations helps do-it-yourselfers who have a modest level of construction experience. Adding a community tool bank also makes this feasible for those who lack the necessary tools and equipment.

5.2.2.3. Task 3: Identify the available risk communication sources in the community

Sources can be categorised as authorities, news media, and peers. These sources are judged in terms of their credibility, which is a combination of expertise and trustworthiness. Perceptions of credibility vary depending upon whether a source is speaking about hazards or hazard adjustments. Official sources are generally the most credible. People look for sources to have impressive credentials, previous experience, or the respect of others. Ethnic minorities trust different types of sources. Research has focused on the perceptions that Mexican Americans, African Americans, and Caucasians have of source characteristics.

Authorities tend to be regarded as credible by the majority of all three ethnic groups. African Americans and Caucasians tend to be more skeptical of the mass media than Mexican Americans. In general, Mexican Americans are more likely than other groups to consider peers to be the most credible sources. There is evidence, however, that the results vary by community. This reflects historical differences in relationships between ethnic groups and authorities in these specific communities.

5.2.2.4. Task 4: Identify the available risk communication channels in the community

Electronic and print media are available in most communities. Using the media is one way to communicate risks to the community. Additional ways include informal face-to-face conversations and formal meetings. A long-term relationship with local businesses sometimes generates contributions to pay for low cost items such as brochures and posters.

5.2.2.5. Task 5: Identify specific audience segments

It is easier and cheaper to develop one communication message for the entire community, but it won't be as effective as tailoring your message to different groups.

5.2.3. Step 3: Mobilise Resources

As an emergency manager, one should perform the following five mobilise resource tasks.

5.2.3.1. Task 1: Obtain the support of senior appointed and elected officials

The manager needs the support of senior officials. They help her/him acquire resources and help put emergency management on the political agenda. Getting this support is also an important step toward obtaining the participation of other government agencies.

5.2.3.2. Task 2: Enlist the participation of other government agencies

No matter how supportive senior officials are, they have limited resources. This means s/he should work with other agencies to share the cost of risk communication. Ensure that each agency is aware of the risk communication programmes being planned by other governmental agencies, non-governmental organisations, and hazardous technological facilities. Gather the resources of multiple agencies within local government. Identify ways s/he can work together to achieve the goals of both organisations.

5.2.3.3. Task 3: Enlist the participation of non-governmental and private sector organisations

Organisations such as the American Red Cross and the Salvation Army play an important role. They help communities prepare for emergencies and recover from disasters. They routinely work with needy families. Consequently, they can identify areas with a high concentration of population that are most vulnerable to disasters. These organisations can also identify methods of assisting households to prepare for emergencies, reduce the vulnerability of their homes, or find safer places to which they can move.

5.2.3.4. Task 4: Work with the mass media

The mass media, with all the television channels, Web sites, newspapers, and radio stations, reach many residents each day. Working with the media allows s/he to get their message out. With more people seeing their message, more people will become aware of the role of emergency management within the community. Also, reporters know their audiences and focus on them. This allows them to target messages to specific audience groups. These groups are defined by gender, age, ethnicity (and language), and socioeconomic status. Reporters do not always consider hazard information to be newsworthy.

5.2.3.5. Task 5: Work with neighbourhood associations and civic organisations

Most communities have many neighbourhood groups and civic organisations whose members are active in their community. These groups work with the community and their members and can help instruct them on the hazards and hazard adjustments. Time is often available for this because many of these organisations want to meet on a regular schedule but do not have enough activities to fill their agendas. Consequently, they are often willing to host speakers whose topics will interest their members.

5.2.4. Step 4: Develop a Programme

As an emergency manager, there are four tasks s/he must perform when developing a programme.

5.2.4.1. Task 1. Staff and train a crisis communication team

Establish a crisis communication team. The team forms a critical link between experts and the population. The team must be able to communicate effectively with both groups. There should be one spokesperson on the team who understands the scientific aspects of the situation and can explain it to everyone at a level they can understand. Spokespersons with technical credentials will generally be considered credible. And spokespersons with previous disaster experience will be seen as credible as well. It also is helpful if team members receive training from public relations experts.

5.2.4.2. Task 2: Establish procedures for maintaining an effective communication flow during an escalating crisis or emergency response

All organisations should establish procedures for coordinating information. It is critical that each organisation receives all the information it needs as promptly as possible. The types of information needed in an escalating crisis depend on the circumstances.

5.2.4.3. Task 3: Develop a comprehensive risk communication programme

The four key factors when designing a message are:

- Personal risk.
- Personal responsibility.
- Guidance for protective action.
- Sources for further information.

One should design messages to address all of these factors. Messages should include any important details but, generally, be short and concise. Too many details can overwhelm people and prevent them from listening. Information should be presented in a way that attracts attention, so people will understand and remember it more easily. Address risk perception but do not over emphasise it. S/he should address risk perception because probabilities are difficult for many to understand.

5.2.4.4. Task 4: Plan to make Effective use of informal communication networks

It is important for you to recognise that people talk to their peers throughout all phases of emergency management. Use these informal networks to increase the level of hazard adjustment adoption. However, friends, relatives, neighbours, and coworkers might not understand a message, or they might not remember the message correctly. To reduce confusion, release information through several channels. Provide many opportunities for people to hear messages so they will retain the common elements of these messages.

5.2.4.5. Task 5: Establish procedures for obtaining feedback from the news media and the public

Feedback is a critical part of any communication process. It provides receivers an opportunity to confirm that they have comprehended the message, to reconcile inconsistencies within or between messages, or to obtain information that is not available in the messages they have received. Feedback is part of informal face-to face discussions, but opportunities for receiving feedback are more limited in public hearings. Public comments frequently are limited to a few minutes at the end of a meeting. The need for feedback is why many experts recommend informal channels of communication.

Therefore, agency procedures that require public hearings should be supplemented by less formal meetings. During emerging crises, reporters might unintentionally distort your message because they didn't quite understand what you were saying. This makes it important to read local newspapers, listen to radio, and view television broadcasts to see if your information is being correctly presented. In addition, you can obtain feedback from citizens via rumor control centers, using a telephone number or a Web site that has been publicised in advance.

5.2.5. Step 5: Implement the Risk Communication Programme

As an emergency manager, there are five tasks one must perform when implementing the risk communication programme.

5.2.5.1. Task 1: Build source credibility by increasing perceptions of expertise and trustworthiness

It is important for personnel from each agency to develop a history of effective job performance that enhances their credibility. This experience is gained during minor incidents, such as minor floods, that cause damage and disruption of normal activities. Credibility is also enhanced by effective performance in public hearings or in meetings with neighbourhood associations and civic organisations. Of course, expertise is only one component of credibility; trustworthiness is also essential. Earn a community's trust by being competent, caring, honourable, and considering outrage factors when working with the public.

5.2.5.2. Task 2: Use a variety of channels to disseminate hazard information

Use not only the news media, but informal channels to communicate your message. Also use opportunities to meet with neighbourhood associations and civic organisations.

5.2.5.3. Task 3: Describe community or facility hazard adjustments being planned or implemented

Inform residents of any actions being taken to reduce the probability of an incident so they understand that their risk is being reduced. Acknowledge that there is no action that can guarantee complete safety. For example, land-use and building construction practices can reduce, but not eliminate, the threat of natural hazards. The same can be said about engineered safety features in connection with technological hazards. In addition, describe actions being taken to facilitate a response to an emergency should one occur.

5.2.5.4. Task 4: Describe feasible household hazard adjustments

Let people know what actions they can take to protect themselves and reduce damage to their homes.

5.2.5.5. Task 5: Evaluate Programme Effectiveness

Set goals for the risk communication programme and determine how they should be measured. It is very common for emergency managers to measure programme effectiveness by reporting the number of meetings attended and the number of brochures distributed. Better measures of effectiveness include increases in the number of households with hazard insurance, family emergency plans, earthquake-prone homes with water heaters strapped to the foundations, and hurricane-prone homes with window shutters.

5.3. Communication During Emergency

An escalating crisis is a situation in which there is a significantly increased probability of an incident occurring that will threaten the public's health, safety, or property. Not everyone will agree that there is a crisis. As a practical matter, a crisis exists if authorities, the news media, or a significant proportion of residents believe there is one. The principle behind this is that "perception is reality." If the news media or local residents believe there is a crisis, then there is a crisis unless authorities can convince them otherwise. Thus, authorities must be prepared to explain specifically why they believe a situation is or is not a crisis.

5.3.1. Step 1: Classify the Situation

One can exert control over people's definition of a situation by defining a system for classifying threat levels. The classification system needs to be established in advance, defined objectively, and agreed to by all responding organisations. By establishing an emergency classification system, authorities commit themselves to taking specific actions when certain criteria are met. With this system, decisions are made based on rational scientific considerations rather than emotion or other considerations.

5.3.2. Step 2: Implement a Risk Communication Programme

Once there is an emergency, authorities will act. Some of the actions will include protecting the population, protecting the environment, and assessing the situation. One of the most important incident management actions is risk communication. As an emergency manager, you must perform six tasks when implementing an emergency response programme.

5.3.2.1. Task 1: Activate the crisis communication team promptly

One need to contact all appropriate authorities. Make sure all communication links are open and all sources of information and expertise are used. Monitor information from other organisations so they can identify any disagreement.

5.3.2.2. Task 2: Determine the appropriate time to release sensitive information

One must determine when to alert others of the danger. Her/his team needs to know when to release information. There are no hard and fast rules about when information should be released. Early information often turns out to be incorrect as the facts are still coming in. However, an early release can enhance your credibility and give them more control. Being the first to break bad news allows you to put the information into an appropriate context. In addition, controlling the timing of a press release can have a significant impact on the amount of attention it receives. A press release distributed on a slow news day might receive more coverage than the same information released on a busy day or on a Friday afternoon. The disadvantage of delaying the release of information is that this can be misinterpreted as a cover-up if the information is leaked. It is also important to respond to reporters' questions when they are aware that something important is happening. Statements of "no comment" are interpreted as meaning authorities are withholding important information.

5.3.2.3. Task 3: Select the communication channels that are appropriate to the situation

An escalating crisis is newsworthy, so you will have little difficulty in obtaining media coverage. Initiate communication with reporters through press releases and press conferences. Press releases give you the most control over the agenda, and interviews with individual reporters provide the least control. You need to ensure reporters are accurately disseminating the information. However, this alone cannot ensure those at risk are receiving, heeding, and comprehending the information they need. You need to promote dialogue through two-way communication, preferably in small groups.

5.3.2.4. Task 4: Maintain source credibility with the news media and the public

Data should be obtained timely and accurately. If the available data is incomplete, you should be honest about what is and is not known. A candid confession of ignorance might be uncomfortable at the time, but it is less dangerous to one's credibility than making up an answer that is later found out to be incorrect. The news media have many sources of information. This is why it is important to respond to reporters when they need information for a deadline. If you do not respond, they will obtain whatever information they can from whatever sources are available at the time.

If you don't have information, it is better to explain that data is being collected, describe how it will be analysed, and indicate when the information will be released. Trust is a major issue. There is little trust in society and what is there can be lost easily. Television anchors tend to be among the few people other than independent scientists that are generally trusted. Television anchors are trusted because they are familiar, authoritative, and have developed a track record of accuracy. You may be stereotyped as a typical bureaucrat. This is the reason why it is important to work with the community on issues before crises arise and publicise your accomplishments.

5.3.2.5. Task 5: Provide timely and accurate information about the hazard to the news media and the public

Press releases should be no longer than two pages with simple short sentences in plain English. They should contain

- A dateline (date and location of release)

- The organisational source (including point of contact) for the information
- A summary lead sentence
- A brief description of any attachments

Press releases should be supplemented by fact sheets, which contain background information. There should be attachments including a biographical summary of the spokesperson and other details about the hazard and official responses. Be prepared to describe the process by which risks are being assessed and what the risks are. In general, it is important to presume the average member of the audience is intelligent but uninformed about environmental risks. Avoid acronyms and technical jargon. Also anticipate the possibility of confrontational tactics by the news media or some members of the public. If confronted with different interpretations, be prepared to calmly restate your scientific qualifications, support your own position, and explain the weaknesses in alternative positions.

5.3.2.6. Task 6: Evaluate performance through post-incident critiques

Organisations must learn from experience. Thus, each incident in which you must disseminate risk information to the news media or the public should be followed by a thorough critique of performance. All members of the crisis communication team should review the goals of the risk communication programme, the event logs kept during the incident, and other available documentation to identify weaknesses in performance. Experiences in drills, exercises, and incidents have demonstrated the importance of focusing on the performance of the organisation rather than the performance of individuals because this enhances a spirit of cooperation. Thus, each participant should be encouraged to follow up on any weaknesses by identifying potential improvements in plans, procedures, and training.

References

Baker, Earl J., "Predicting Response to Hurricane Warnings: A Reanalysis of Data fromFour Studies", *Mass Emergencies,* 1979.

., "Hurricane Evacuation Behavior", *International Journal of Mass Emergencies and Disasters,* 1991.

., "Public Response to Hurricane Probability Forecasts", *Professional Geographer,* 1995.

., "Hurricane Evacuation in the United States", Pp. 306-319 in Storms Volume I. London: Routledge, 2000.

Baker, Jay, "Warning and Evacuation in Hurricanes Elena and Kate", *Tallahassee,* FL: Department of Geography, Florida State University, 1987.

Balluz, L., L. Schieve, T. Holmes, S. Kiezak, J. Malilay, "Predictors for People's Response to a Tornado Warning: Arkansas, 1 March 1997", *Disasters,* 2000.

Fitzpatrick, Colleen and Dennis S. Mileti, "Perception and Response to Aftershock Warnings During the Emergency Period", Pp. 75-83 in *The Loma Prieta Earthquake: Studies of Short-Term Impacts,* Monograph No. 50, edited by R.

Bolin. Boulder, CO: Natural Hazards Research and Applications Information Center, Institute of Behavioral Science, University of Colorado, 1990.

Lindell, Michael K., Ronald W. Perry, and Marjorie R. Greene, "Race and Disaster Warning Response." Seattle, WA: Battelle Human Affairs Research Centers, 1980.

Mack, Raymond W. and George W. Baker, "The Occasion Instant: The Structure of Social Responses to Repeated Air Raid Warnings", Washington, D.C.: National Research Council, National Academy of Sciences, 1961.

Mileti, Dennis S. and Paul W. O'Brien, "Warnings During Disaster: Normalizing Communicated Risk", *Social Problems,* 1992.

CHAPTER 6

Assessing Risk and Vulnerability

6.1. Introduction

Understanding risks and their causes is important in dealing with disasters. People's knowledge of what makes a person or a community more vulnerable than another determines the steps they can take to reduce their risk. Society takes collective action to protect itself against risks and has been successful in doing so. Reducing the risk of disease has been one of the greatest social achievements of the last century and a half. Average life expectancy for someone born in Europe in 1841 was 35 yeas. Now in most high income countries it is over 70 years, and over 50 years even in the 40 poorest countries. Most of this is due to the virtual disappearance over this time of mortality due to infectious disease. Societies appear to become generally safer and less tolerant of risks as they become more technologically advanced. And yet some technological advances bring with them increased risks: the automobile has cost many lives.

Energy supplies and industries introduce new hazards, and so on. The benefits of new technologies appear to outweigh the risks they bring and we as a society seem to tolerate different risks for different reasons. The demand for increased safety in the home and safety in the workplace continue. As the risks diminish from common events like disease, the risks posed by extraordinary events, like natural hazards assume a greater significance. The level of safety that is being pursued is not specific.

In many cases it is far more cost-effective to prevent disasters from occurring beforehand than to recover from them afterwards. In developing countries, the United Nations Development Program is promoting the goal of sustainable development, and it is argued that disaster awareness considerations should be incorporated into all development programming and planning, both to protect the development process and to reduce the risk of wasting scarce development resources. The UNDP and DHA also have a growing involvement in projects specifically orientated towards disaster mitigation. These projects are prompted by growing awareness of the risks faced and increasing realization that some level of protection is possible.

The term risk refers to the expected losses from a given hazard to a given element at risk, over a specified future time period. According to the way in which the element at risk is defined, the risk may be measured in terms of expected economic loss, or in terms of numbers of lives lost or the extent of physical damage to property. Specific risk is also used for financial losses to property, where it usually refers to the ratio of the cost of repair or reinstatement of the property to the cost of total replacement. Frequently the shorter term 'risk' is used to refer to what are strictly 'specific risks.'

6.2. Risk Assessment and Evaluation

The overall task of risk management must include both an estimation of the magnitude of a particular risk and an evaluation of how important to us the risk is. The process of risk management therefore has two parts:

a) *Risk essessment*: The scientific quantification of risk from data and understanding of the processes involved.

b) *Risk evaluation*: The social and political judgement of the importance of various risks by the individuals and communities that face them. This involves trading off perceived risks against potential benefits and also includes balancing scientific judgements against other factors and beliefs.

In order to understand a risk and to compare different risks, scientists and economists usually try to quantify it. This is done by gathering data on the effects of various hazards that cause the risk and on the basis of statistical analysis, predicting the probability of future events. The identification of causes, effects and the understanding of the processes of disaster occurrence are critical to the assessment of future risks. The accuracy of risk quantification depends to a considerable extent on the amount of data available. The number of events on which information is available has to be large enough to be statistically significant. In addition the quality or reliability of the data has to be adequate. These factors all pose problems for the risk assessor who has to identify 'confidence limits' or range of doubt over any future risk estimations offered. Some risks are easier to quantify than others. The risks of the effects of minor floods and small earthquakes are easier to predict than catastrophic ones because they have happened more often and there is more data on their occurrence. Likewise the recurrence of droughts may be predicted on the basis of historical experience. On the other hand, risks of events that have not yet happened, such as the melt-down of a nuclear reactor for instance, have no past statistics and so have to be estimated from probabilities and forecasts.

6.3. Vulnerability and Risk Assessment

The risk of natural disasters is something everybody face. The magnitude of risk varies person to person and the place they live and work they do. How important the risk of natural disasters is compared with other risks in the lives of people will determine whether they do anything about it and how much they do. Awareness of the risk by the public in general and perception of how it compares to other risks will determine society's attitudes about reducing it. Flood prevention planners in Brazil, for example can learn a lot from a detailed analysis of a major flood in Bangladesh. The analysis of flood statistics world wide can help define risk levels and characteristics of return periods of floods in individual locations where specific data is scanty. People who live in the more vulnerable building type are more at risk from a future earthquake than the others. The importance of studying the effects of hazards in order to understand risk and to make effective decisions on risk mitigation should be clearly understood. To understand risk it is necessary not just to study the casualties, but also to study those people who were not affected. Risk needs to be defined in terms of the probability of the effects and the proportion of the total population affected.

Risk can be described and expressed in a number of ways. One standard method is to count all the people exposed to a particular risk and divide this number by the number of people who have actually experienced the hazard over a defined time span. If the number of people who travel by train in any one year is ten million and ten people are killed on average each year, then the annual risk of being killed in train travel is one in one million.

There is no one standard way of defining the population exposed to a risk, so statistical expressions of risk need to be carefully defined and explained for them to be useful. Gross levels of risk, taking the number of deaths from hat cause, divided by some estimate of the population exposed can give the type of approximate ranking of probability of death to an individual by different causes. This gives some idea of how disaster risk to an individual compares with other risks, and how disaster risk may vary from place to place. Those living in poorer quality houses are more at risk than people who live in strong seismically resistant houses. But to define the exact seismic zones and the exact number of people in houses of different seismic resistance requires much more detailed analysis. Some of these types of analysis are described in examples given later in this module.

Disaster risks are unlikely to be considered important in a community that faces much greater everyday threats of disease and food shortages - even if disaster risk is quite significant it is unlikely to compare with the risk of child mortality in a society with minimal primary health care. Villages in the hazardous mountain valleys of Northern Pakistan, regularly afflicted by floods, earthquakes and landslides, do not perceive disaster mitigation to be one of their priorities. Their priorities are protection against the greater risks of disease and irrigation failures.

By contrast, communities in much less hazardous environments, living in much less vulnerable houses, in California for example, initiate disaster mitigation programs, because relative to diseases and other risks which are very low, disasters are perceived as important. The level of disaster risk relative to other comparable risks is important in determining whether a community or an individual takes action to reduce it. The amount of resources available to invest in disaster mitigation and the value of infrastructure to be protected also determines how readily a community will carry out disaster mitigation.

As societies develop economically, disaster mitigation is likely to assume greater importance to them. Development itself can increase the likelihood of disasters. Industrial development can bring new hazards; improved health care and economic growth can cause demographic changes, migration and concentrations of population. The amount, which could be lost in a disaster grows, as resources are accumulated. Better public health and improvements in other sectors are likely to reduce comparative risk levels in everyday threats, so that the risks posed by extraordinary events assume a greater significance. As societies become richer more resources can be made available to invest in some degree of protection. Protection of the development process itself becomes a disaster mitigation issue.

Development programs and developing countries are the most important arenas for disaster mitigation. Societies in transition from an agrarian to an industrialised economy will be developing an awareness of some of the new environmental risks they face, and an understanding of some of the possible means of protecting themselves from them. But at the same time, the development process has the potential to damage or destroy protection provided by traditional ways of doing things - through siting and land-use, building practice, community defenses or agricultural practices. Replacing these with modern techniques may be a very costly option. Thus an appropriate risk reduction strategy for a developing country has to include an understanding of traditional risk mitigation techniques and should build on them rather than replace them.

6.3.1. Perception of Risk

The key to a successful programme to reduce risk is to understand the importance that society attaches to the hazards that confront it, that is to say on its own perception of risk. Decisions have to be made about risks, even if that decision is to do nothing about it. In most societies, several groups are involved in these decisions.

In principle, experts gather the scientific and socio-economic evidence and give technical advice to the politicians, who then legislate and regulate for the benefit and with the implicit agreement of the general public. In practice, of course, things do not very often work out that way. Assessing risk from the available data is not always as helpful as the experts would like. Politicians can have interests and objectives in decisions other than the simple consideration of risk mitigation, and the general public may not see things the same way as either the experts or the politicians. Decisions are made and actions are taken according to the way that risks are perceived. Perception of risk can differ from one group to another. Experts like to use statistics. But most other people are less comfortable with statistical concepts and prefer to base perceptions of risk on a range of other values, philosophies, concepts and calculations.

Perception of risk has been an important area of psychological research. The mental process of evaluating risk-makingmaking sense out of a complex collection of different types of information-tends to differ significantly between individuals and groups. Rules of judgement may be evolved within one group which can lead to valid and consistent decisions, but which may be significantly different from those of another group or individual that has used different patterns of thought to evaluate the same set of facts. Similar differences exist between the individuals within any group.

6.3.2. Risk and the Media

An important element in the psychology of risk perception is the 'availability' of information. The mental strategy for decision-making is to match a situation under review with the information that is most readily available and easily recalled. The more 'available' the information on a given event, the more likely it is judged that the event will occur. Things that happen often are easy to remember. The frequency of reporting the occurrence of an event like a natural hazard will increase its perception. But many other factors also influence recall-mental 'availability' of information-and thus perception of risk. Attributes of drama, context and experience influence recall. Dramatic information rich in death and disaster tends to be highly memorable. For most people, personal contact with hazards is fairly rare and so knowledge of them is acquired more through the news media than from first-hand experience. The way the media report hazards is extremely influential in risk perception. The media tend to concentrate on the more unusual and dramatic happenings in its reporting, and so these events are often perceived to be more frequent than they actually are. Research has been carried out in the USA and a number of other industrialised countries into risk perception. Experiments asking various groups of people to judge the frequency of various causes of death, like diseases, accidents and natural hazards, show that judgements are moderately accurate with a number of distinct biases.

6.3.3. Risk Perception with less Information

Populations without regular exposure to news media may underestimate the environmental risks they face. There is evidence that risk perception is considerably influenced by availability of information. Some societies without access to information on hazards appear to have lower perceptions of the risk of natural hazards that might strike them. Research with a range of different subject groups has shown that an individual's background and experience-variables like technological familiarity and social grouping-can affect risk perception considerably and quite selectively.

There have been no psychological studies of perception of risk among groups much less exposed to media coverage or groups with much higher actual risks of natural disasters comparable with that described above, but a number of social studies of less-informed communities facing high risks have concluded that the individuals are probably more at risk from hazards than they realise. Rural communities or societies with little formal education may have less information available to them on which to make risk decisions. Their perception of risk is likely to be shaped more by personal experience, local and recent events and verbal folklore than by media presentation of risks. Information horizons-the distance from which they are brought news and the length of history they have available to them-may not encompass the rarer events that pose their major threat. Their familiarity with hazards-particularly with return periods longer than their lifetimes-may be minimal and causes of hazards and recognition of danger signs may be beyond their experience. A common ingredient of disaster mitigation programs is a public education program to increase disaster awareness. This is not only to increase perception of risk where is judged too low, it is also to educate the public that disasters are preventable and to encourage them to participate in protecting themselves.

6.3.4. Qualitative Aspects

An important finding of the research in risk perception is that the abstraction of risk is more easily accepted than the personalization of risk. "It'll never happen to me", is a common attitude in both richer and poorer societies. Complex issues relating to risk and to the possibility of personal injury are handled psychologically by rejecting them. The risk of death or injury to a group of people, even a group that includes the individual is more readily accepted than the risk to the individual personally. Familiar risks confronted many times like driving a car on mountain roads or crossing a dormant volcano may well make this risk discountable, or of lower perception. Inescapable risks may be completely rejected and virtually ignored. In general, the research into perception shows that people evaluate risks through a number of subjective concepts and beliefs in a multi-dimensional way. The quantitative aspects of risk are less important than some of the qualitative attributes of the risk - the image of a particular risk and the conjecture associated with it.

Disasters that cause large numbers of deaths are more dreadful than low-fatality catastrophes. Perception of risk appears closely related to the dread factor, and only generally related to exposure levels or to personal familiarity. High levels of perceived risk are usually associated with desires or actions to reduce risk and with support to the community and its representatives to reduce risks on their behalf. It is also clear that increased access to factual information can increase perception of risk and thereby also reduce acceptance of risk and what is considered 'safe'.

6.3.5. Acceptable Levels of Risks

Very high levels of perceived risk are associated with actions to reduce risk-when people think the risk of the volcano erupting is too high, they move. At some level the risk becomes unacceptable. The concept of risk tolerance and the thresholds of unacceptability are what determine, ultimately, whether public money is voted through for a flood dike project or whether people comply with building regulations to make their houses earthquake resistant. Many risks are also associated with benefits. Living close to a volcano may bringbenefit of fertile igneous soils for good agriculture. The risks associated with chest X-rays and driving to work are generally considered acceptable because the benefits are immediately obvious. Generally, the exposure to natural and environmental hazards does not have any specific benefit associated with it: the exposure is a simple consequence of living or working in a particular location. This can have the effect of making such risks less acceptable than those from which some benefit is obtained. Generally the acceptable levels of risk appear to increase according to the benefits derived from being exposed to it.

Some risks are entered into voluntarily and a distinction is sometimes made between voluntary and involuntary risk. Many recreational activities and sports, involve considerable levels of personal risk entered into voluntarily. Indeed the thrill of the risk is part of the enjoyment of the recreation. The benefits of the risk outweigh the costs and so the perception of the risk is reduced; i.e. the level that is deemed acceptable is much higher than a risk that is imposed from outside or involuntary.

6.3.6. Management

The level of risk from a natural hazard to an individual is far less than the risk posed to a whole community. The chance of an individual being caught in an area randomly hit by a natural hazard, for example, is relatively small, but if the area of jurisdiction of an authority - a district, a province, or a whole country, is larger, the chances of being affected by a disaster are proportionately higher. For this reason it is commonly argued that management of risk is more important to the community than to the individual. Many risks are managed at a community level rather than at an individual level. Not only are the community's resources greater, there is also more motivation to tackle the risk. Legislation, large-scale engineering structures and installations for hazard reduction, and establishment of safety organisations are all community-level initiatives for reducing risks. Institutions which can influence the safety and protection of the community include the legislature, government departments and administrative bodies, industrial organisations and many others. Non-governmental organisations may also act on behalf of the community and may be involved in assisting risk reduction activities, being voluntarily answerable to the community.

Different countries and social groups have different attitudes towards safety and community protection. The greatest difference is likely to be in the degree of public participation envisaged, either formally, through public enquires and protection drills or informally, through pressures of public opinion expressed in the media. Actual techniques of risk mitigation are described in more detail in the Disaster Mitigation module of this series.

6.3.7. Technological Hazards

Historically, the perception of risk, and thus society's motivation for reducing it, is dependent to some extent on exposure to the risk-i.e. its probability of occurrence. Generally, however, the 'dread factor' which is related to the scale of the potential catastrophe has a greater impact. There is little doubt that disasters are formidable and newsworthy events because of the number of deaths that can occur even though higher levels of risk may be represented by losses on a smaller scale. For example, leukemia or diabetes may be the greater killers in aggregate, but the fact that they kill individually and without drama makes them less "newsworth" and less alarming. Disasters kill numbers of people at once-an airplane crash causes more horror than an equivalent number of the more frequent car crashes because larger numbers of passengers are killed in a single event. The size of a disaster then, represented by its number of fatalities, is almost as important for its perception as its frequency of occurrence.

6.3.8. Using Risk in Decision-making

The estimation of probable future losses is a matter of increasing interest to those concerned with development planning or with the management of facilities or public administration in hazard-prone regions. Future loss estimates are of interest to those responsible for development and physical planning on an urban or regional scale, particularly where planning decisions can have an effect on future losses; for the same reason they are of interest to economic planners on a national or international scale. Loss estimates are also of interest to those who own or manage large numbers of buildings or other vulnerable facilities and to the insurance and reinsurance companies, which insure those facilities. Equally, loss estimates are of importance to those responsible for civil protection, relief, and emergency services to enable adequate contingency plans to be prepared; and they concern also those who draft building regulations or codes of practice for construction, whose task is to ensure that adequate protection is provided by those codes at minimum cost. The type of loss estimates required depends on the user: for some purposes estimates of physical losses - of buildings, infrastructure and equipment may be the primary need, while in other cases the numbers of human casualties, and numbers of homeless may be equally important. For long-term development planning, aspects such as economic loss and social disruption also need to be estimated.

Taking measures to reduce the effects of future hazards is becoming increasingly common in planning the future development of cities or regions, which have a history of disasters. Preparedness Planning involves contingency measures to cope with the emergency when it occurs and Mitigation Planning involves the long-term control of land use, building stock quality and other measures to reduce the impact of a hazard when it eventually strikes. Fundamental to these planning processes is an understanding of what to expect. This needs to be quantified, if only in a crude and approximate way, in terms of the degree of risk faced, the size of event that is likely, and the consequences of an event if it occurs.

6.3.9. Types of Losses

Risk is quantified in most of the examples given so far in terms of loss of life. It is generally accepted that saving life is the highest priority of disaster mitigation and preparedness. Furthermore, deaths are absolute and can be counted more easily than injuries. It is therefore relatively straightforward to compare smoking and flood risks in terms of number of people killed. However, many other parameters of disaster consequences may be of equal or more practical value to us. For the medical profession, for example, prediction of injuries are more useful than fatality estimates because injury risk relates to resources needed for treatment. Whatever the ultimate purpose of the analysis, the calculation of risk generally needs to consider several types of loss. The most common parameter of loss, and the one most easily dealt with, is economic cost. Cost is widely used because many types of loss can be converted into economic cost. It is a currency for considering a wide range of effects. Effects, which are considered in terms of economic costs are known as tangible losses. But there are a range of other effects resulting from disasters which are important but which cannot be converted into a monetary equivalent, and these are referred to as intangible losses. A full consideration of risk would include a complete range of effects, both tangible and intangible, and of several qualitatively different types.

6.3.9.1. Presentation

Risk or specific risk is defined as the average rate of loss or 'attrition rate'. While this is useful for estimating losses over a long period of time, it can give a misleading idea of the nature of the risk from natural hazards. Most of the losses from these events actually occur through infrequent large single events, rather than in the form of a slow continuous process of destruction. A variety of different methods have been developed for the presentation of risk to help overcome this difficulty.

However, such relationships always show aggregated losses for a large region and period of time. They do not help to identify the geographical distribution of damage, for which risk mapping is needed. Risk maps attempt to show the spatial or geographical distribution of expected losses from one or more natural hazards. Because of the way natural hazards occur, the presentation of annual risk is not necessarily the most useful, and several different ways of presenting losses are commonly used including:

6.3.9.2. Estimation of rare events

Natural hazards are extreme cases of normal events; a hurricane is an extreme wind, a destructive earthquake is a large version of the energy released by geological processes that are occurring everyday, a flood is the result of extreme precipitation or storm, or tidal conditions. Extreme meteorological, hydrological or geophysical events pose threats to the human-made environment and to individuals. By definition, extreme events are rare. The more extreme and severe an event is, the rarer it is. Extreme occurrences of natural hazards are difficult to predict. They occur irregularly - there are very few clearly identifiable patterns of occurrence of natural hazards (although studies are beginning to show that some longer term patterns may be discernible) - and in the short term they appear almost random. Because they happen rarely, there is not a large number of extreme cases in the databases, and statistical forecasting based on past occurrences is unreliable. A volcano that has erupted only once in the past century may erupt once every thousand years or it may have an average eruption rate of once every twenty years and its recent quiescence just happens to be an unusually long gap in its eruption frequency.

6.3.9.3. Hazard mapping

Hazard recurrence probability varies from place to place, and one of the most important ways of understanding the risk faced by any community or region is to use the available data to plot hazard maps. According to the type of hazard, various types of hazard maps may be useful. A map of expected maximum site parameter over a specified time period, as shown for an earthquake hazard in map 1 of figure 6, may be useful for some purposes. For other purposes the probability of the occurrence of an event exceeding a certain magnitude may be more useful.

Flood hazard is often mapped so that the maximum extent of floods with different return periods are superimposed on each other. The hazard map in figure 8 shows the flood hazard for Manila plotted to show the areas inundated by the expected annual flood and the larger areas expected to be inundated by floods with average return periods of 10 years, 20 years and 100 years.

Volcanic hazards are less easily quantified, but areas at greatest risk can easily be identified. The scale of mapping appropriate for hazard maps depends both on the use and the amount of data available. Knowledge of the spatial distribution of some hazards, such as earthquakes, landslides and floods has reached the level at which variations in risk within a small community can be mapped. Such micro-zoning maps have an important role in land-use planning. Micro-zoning maps can be based on a single event of a single hazard, multiple events of a single hazard, or they can attempt to combine the impact of several different hazards.

6.4. Vulnerability

Vulnerability is the propensity of things to be damaged by a hazard. People's lives and health are at risk directly from the destructive effects of the hazard. Their incomes and livelihood are at risk because of the destruction of the buildings, crops, livestock or equipment, which these depend on. Each type of hazard puts a somewhat different set of elements at risk. Most of disaster mitigation work is focused on reducing vulnerability, and in order to act to reduce vulnerability, development planners need an understanding of which elements are most at risk from the principal hazards, which have been identified.

Vulnerability is defined as the degree of loss to a given element at risk (or set of elements) resulting from a given hazard at a given severity level. (The distinction between this definition and that of risk is important to note. Risk combines the expected losses from all levels of hazard severity, taking account also of their occurrence probability). The vulnerability of an element is usually expressed as a percentage loss (or as a value between 0 to 1) for a given hazard severity level. The measure of loss used depends on the element at risk, and accordingly may be measured as a ratio of the numbers of killed or injured to the total population, as a repair cost or as the degree of physical damage defined on an appropriate scale. In a large number of elements, like building stock, it may be defined in terms of the proportion of buildings experiencing some particular level of damage.

6.4.1. Reducing Vulnerability

It is sometimes argued that using risk concepts in disaster mitigation is too hazard-specific. In a classic risk analysis, the hazard is first identified, then the probability of that hazard occurring is estimated, the vulnerability that relates to that hazard is then identified, and finally action is taken to reduce vulnerability. In this way of doing things, if a hazard happens that has not been foreseen, the disaster mitigation program may not protect against it. It is clearly impossible to predict every disaster hazard. Any society faces a wide range of potential hazards - one thing that characterises disasters is that however carefully they are planned for, they are always surprising. Yet many of the elements of the vulnerability for different hazards are similar.

The soundest defense against disasters is a society that is generally less vulnerable. Although each hazard works in ways that may selectively damage elements with different characteristics - a flood threatens people in the valleys more than on the high ground, hurricanes blow down lightweight houses but not solid ones - in general the defenses of a community are roughly the same. A strong economy is the best defense against disaster.

The objective of programs to reduce vulnerability should be to create a robust society, resistant to hazardous influences in general, rather than one rather narrowly protected against one type of event - an earthquake or a flood. The underlying reasons that make communities vulnerable are the same for any type of disaster, and if it is possible to tackle some of the root causes of vulnerability, the robustness of that society will be improved. The linkage between disasters and economic development is strong. It is the subject of the Disasters and Development module in this training course. The most vulnerable societies are those weakest economically.

Similarly the most vulnerable members of each society are those that are economically marginalised. The worst locations to live, the steep landslideprone hillsides, the riverside flood plains, are the places that the poorest find to live. Houses built for minimal cash cost are most vulnerable to wind storms or earthquakes. The underlying mechanisms that cause vulnerability have to be well understood in order to reduce it. Vulnerability is largely a developmental issue, and vulnerability reduction needs to be carried out within a developmental context. Protection of their resources and improvements in the economic potential of a community or group may be as critical as reducing their vulnerability.

6.5. Disaster Mitigation Options

Disaster mitigation measures take a variety of different forms, discussed in more detail in the Disaster Mitigation module in this training course. These include engineering measures to build more hazard-resistant structures, physical planning to locate important facilities away from hazards, economic measures to protect earnings, management structures to ensure protection measures are carried through and societal measures to encourage the public to support mitigation measures.

Measures like establishing building codes for new construction, strengthening existing buildings, land-use controls, and improving preparedness planning are generally costly to apply, whether it is individuals, private companies or the general tax-payer who will ultimately be responsible. Equally, it can be costly to fail to apply any mitigation measures in an area of known hazard, both in financial and in human terms. As a general rule, it can be expected that the higher the level of protection, the higher the cost of protection will be; but against this can be set the lower cost of future losses.

6.5.1. Risk Assessment

When development projects, like any other projects, are undertaken without regard for the risks of future hazards, the investment level considered adequate for the program may be insufficient to protect it during its lifetime. When making a cutting for a road, for example, a steeper angle for the cutting is cheaper than a shallow one, so an efficient engineer will choose the steepest angle that the soil will bear to minimize the cost. If however, the possibility of an extremely heavy rainfall or strong ground tremor is not considered, the cutting will collapse and the road may be buried or washed away. The investment in the road may be wasted for the lack of the extra cost to widen the cutting angle a few extra degrees to give a safety margin against natural hazards.

One important procedure that has been proposed is to include disaster potential in the economic analysis of a project design. The extra costs of protection, it is counter-argued, would make some projects not economically viable. However, the basic argument for integrating disaster awareness into development planning is that it is wasteful not to do so.

6.5.2. Cost Benefit Analysis

The most widely used method for choosing between alternative investments designed to achieve some socially desirable outcome is cost-benefit analysis. This method has been widely used for assessing hazard mitigation projects in floods and other hazards, particularly major engineering projects. At its simplest, the idea is that all the benefits of the project are computed in financial terms, the costs are then deducted, and the difference is the value of the project. All projects with a positive value are worthwhile, but in a situation with a number of possible alternative projects and with limited resources available for investment, the project or projects with the highest value, or alternatively the highest rate of return on initial investment, are chosen. In most cases this simple idea is complicated by the fact that the investments are made some time in advance of the benefits being felt, so that some rate of trade-off between present cost and future benefit has to be introduced. This is generally dealt with by introducing a social discount rate, which is considered to reflect society's preference for present benefits over future benefits, and for which a consistent value is used in all project evaluations. All future costs and benefits are discounted by the use of this rate. This method can be used in comparing alternative strategies to protect against hazards if, for example the cost is taken as the additional project cost solely related to providing hazard resistance, while the benefits are the reduction in future losses, in terms of building damage, loss of life and other incidental losses, which result from the improved resistance.

6.5.3. Costing Saved Lives

The most important aspect of many disaster mitigation strategies is likely to be that they will save lives. Evaluating which programmes will save most lives is therefore an important output for risk assessment. Some analysts extend the technique of cost-benefit analysis to include the saving of life in its calculation. This is difficult for most people to come to terms with as it involves equating a human life with a financial value, which appears both illogical and morally questionable. Where life saving is to be evaluated in financial terms, the most widely used method of evaluating human life loss is the human capital approach, in which a life is valued in accordance with its potential for future productivity. At its simplest, the monetary value of an individual's life is the discounted sum of all of his or her expected future earnings. The advantage of this approach is that it is relatively simple to calculate. The method has been used in quantifying the benefits of lifesaving programs, for instance the mandatory use of seat belts in automobiles. But distinguishing between the value of different individuals lives on the basis of their earning power is liable to lead to quite unacceptable decisions; for example, it could be computed that there was a zero or even negative loss in the collapse of an old people's home. Similarly the lives of people living on low incomes would be given a lower value. Thus alternative means of appraising options are preferred.

Cost-benefit analysis was originally developed as a tool for evaluating development projects - and work best when the costs and the benefits are calculated in the same terms. But disaster mitigation projects are not solely about economic benefits. The risk parameters being considered are multidimensional, as listed earlier. Their benefits are measured not only financially, but in other terms as well, such as lives saved, injuries prevented, social disruption avoided, and environmental impact reduced. The difficulties of cost-benefit analysis in dealing with saving life shows the problems with a unidimensional approach to risk analysis. Risk analysis that presents risk to life in one equation, economic losses in other and even further dimensions of the problem including environmental impact and the rest separately is still useful. It allows us to make informed decisions. Procedures which prescribe decisions appear far less useful than those that provide information to assist decisions to be made.

6.5.4. Goal-orientated Risk Reduction

Cost-benefit analysis chooses the appropriate level of protection according to a minimum cost criterion; in other words it is assumed that the best level of protection to choose is that which minimises overall cost. It has been shown above that acceptable levels of risk are decided by societies on the basis of perceived risk, and that perceived risk is only partly determined by the actual exposure level. Priorities are assigned and preferences made on the basis of a wide range of cultural influences. Where a community is capable of agreeing what levels of consequences it would find acceptable (or in fact defining the consequences it would find unacceptable) these criteria can be used to define the appropriate level of protection. The community is effectively defining its goals or the target levels of risk it would like to achieve at some future date - the exact level of risk may be unimportant.

Another is to try to determine an acceptable rate of trade of between life-safety and capital cost, again with reference to other areas of human activity in which money is spent to protect life. These procedures will be further discussed below.

6.5.4.1. Balanced risk criterion

The approach to risk reduction using the balanced risk criterion attempts to equalise the levels of risk, which are accepted in society in a range of comparable activities. As in the studies of risk described in the first section of this module, risks of death to an individual can be grouped into two general categories - those associated with voluntary activities, and those associated with involuntary activities, and into further sub-groups of similar risks, like natural disasters, transportation, technological and so on. It has been suggested for instance that the acceptable risk from technological systems from which considerable benefits are obtained approaches that due to disease in society as a whole, while that from uncontrollable (and totally non-beneficial) natural disasters may be 1,000 to 10,000 times lower.

6.5.4.2. Cost-effectiveness criterion

An alternative decision-making criterion is available which incorporates both economic costs and life-safety, but without making an explicit valuation of human life. For a range of possible strategies, the financial costs and benefits are assembled, but without including a valuation of human life. The expected benefits in terms of saved human lives, and saved injuries, are calculated separately. The financial cost per saved life is also calculated, or the marginal cost in comparing one level of protection with an alternative adjacent one. Decision-makers are then faced with choosing between the projects on the basis of these separate attributes, and may use the cost per saved life as an indicator of the cost effectiveness of a particular policy in terms of life saving.

6.6. Conclusion

The quantification of risks, future losses, and the costs and benefits of mitigation programmes, though offering valuable information, does not lead to any clear-cut guidance for the development planner on which is the optimum risk-reduction strategy to choose. The costs and the cost-effectiveness of alternative strategies are a necessary part of the set of factors, which need to be considered. But the intangibles, by their nature, cannot be quantified, yet they must be given proper consideration.

Further, the actual degree of risk and benefit must be judged against the perceived risk, as indicated by the importance, which the community attaches to any proposed expenditure on mitigation. The distribution of costs and benefits among different sections of society has also to be taken into account. Those who will pay and those who will benefit are not always the same people. Some people, such as landowners or property owners may appear to lose more than they gain from mitigation strategies designed to protect the lives and incomes of the poorest and must vulnerable. It is possible to modify cost-benefit analysis so as to identify costs and benefits to different groups, but this exercise can lead to such a mass of data as to be unintelligible.

References

Burton, I., Kates, R.W. and White, G.F., *The Environment as Hazard, Second Edition,* New York/London: Guilford Press, 1993.

Carter, N., *Disaster Management, a disaster Manager's Handbook,* Asian Development Bank, Manilla, 1991.

Coburn, A.W., Spence, R.J.S. and Pomonis, A., "Vulnerability and Risk Assessment", *UNDP Disaster Management Training Program,* 1991.

Freeman, P.K., L. Martin, J. Linnerooth-Bayer, R. Mechler, K. Warner and G. Pflug, "Disaster Risk Management: Financial Strategies for Natural Disaster Reconstruction", *Regional Policy Dialogue on National Systems for Comprehensive Disaster Management,* Washington DC, Inter-American, Development Bank, 2002.

Kelly, P.M. and W.N. Adger, "Theory and Practice in Assessing Vulnerability to Climate Change and Facilitating Adaptation. Climatic Change, 2000.

Smit, B., I. Burton, R.J.T. Klein and R. Street, "The Science of Adaptation: A Framework for Assessment", *Mitigation and Adaptation Strategies for Global Change,* 1999.

CHAPTER 7

Disaster Management in India

7.1. Introduction

Developing countries are becoming increasingly aware of the importance of disaster management systems, and increasing efforts are being made to streamline preparedness, response and recovery mechanisms at all levels. It is well known that many developing countries, including India, are not always well-prepared to deal with disasters. A lack of well-developed disaster management plans results in a severe loss of human life, animal life and property, which could be saved if the necessary mechanisms were in place. A lot needs to be done to improve the situation.

After independence India began a process of rapid industrialisation. It inevitably lacked some framework conditions, such as an understanding of the risks of chemical hazards. Implementation of safety procedures, including regulatory approaches, soon followed and institutions such as the National Safety Council (NSCI) were created. There was much to do. The Bhopal disaster in 1984 did much to focus more attention on the need for a holistic approach to technology disaster management, and the role of ordinary people in emergencies.

The government took several important measures, with major legislative changes and stronger institutional mechanisms. It set up Crisis Groups at central, state, district and local levels. NSCI took the APELL process as a model, promoting awareness and training projects covering both hazardous materials transport and fixed installations. India is also vulnerable to natural disasters. While well-established mechanisms for response, relief and rehabilitation were in place, major events such as the Orissa super-cyclone in 1999 and the Bhuj earthquake in 2001 emphasised the need for a comprehensive approach to mitigation and prevention, for natural and man-made disasters.

A national Advisory Committee and Technical Core Group was set up for periodical review, guidance and technical consultation. In 2002 the first national APELL Centre opened at NSCI headquarters in Mumbai. It was the first centre of this sort in the world. The first projects started in 1992 in six HRIAs, also drawing on international collaboration from UNEP, USAID and WEC. In 2004 an APELL sub-centre opened in Haldia. A manual on cyclone emergency preparedness was prepared.

Practical experience at local level has facilitated-and has in turn been facilitated by-national legislation such as the law setting up crisis groups and safety management in general. Crisis groups at district and local level require training and support tools so there is an ongoing role for training organisations such as NSCI and its offshoots like NAC. Finally, the programme has pinpointed the need to treat transport as a priority issue, linking various locations in the hazardous materials chain across the country.

The experience has also aroused much interest abroad, notably in China, South Africa, Jordan and Brazil, underlining the need to share experience internationally. Emergency prevention and preparedness is a complex issue, and industrialising countries need to address the matter as an integral part of a larger sustainable development agenda. Experience in countries such as India can do much to streamline the process elsewhere, with growing pressures to better address disaster issues.

7.2. Policy Mechanisms

The institutional and policy mechanisms for carrying out response, relief and rehabilitation have been well-established since Independence. These mechanisms have proved to be robust and effective insofar as response, relief and rehabilitation are concerned. At the national level, the Ministry of Home Affairs is the nodal Ministry for all matters concerning disaster management.

The Central Relief Commissioner (CRC) in the Ministry of Home Affairs is the nodal officer to coordinate relief operations for natural disasters. The CRC receives information relating to forecasting/warning of a natural calamity from India Meteorological Department (IMD) or from Central Water Commission of Ministry of Water Resources on a continuing basis.

The Ministries/Departments/Organisations concerned with the primary and secondary functions relating to the management of disasters include: India Meteorological Department, Central Water Commission, Ministry of Home Affairs, Ministry of Defence, Ministry of Finance, Ministry of Rural Development, Ministry of Urban Development, Department of Communications, Ministry of Health, Ministry of Water Resources, Ministry of Petroleum, Department of Agriculture & Cooperation. Ministry of Power, Department of Civil Supplies, Ministry of Railways, Ministry of Information and Broadcasting, Planning Commission, Cabinet Secretariat, Department of Surface Transport, Ministry of Social Justice, Department of Women and Child Development, Ministry of Environment and Forest, Department of Food. Each Ministry/Department/Organisation nominate their nodal officer to the Crisis Management Group chaired by Central Relief Commissioner. The nodal officer is responsible for preparing sectoral Action Plan/Emergency Support Function Plan for managing disasters.

National Crisis Management Committee (NCMC): Cabinet Secretary, who is the highest executive officer, heads the NCMC. Secretaries of all the concerned Ministries /Departments as well as organisations are the members of the Committee The NCMC gives direction to the Crisis Management Group as deemed necessary. The Secretary, Ministry of Home Affairs is responsible for ensuring that all developments are brought to the notice of the NCMC promptly. The NCMC can give directions to any Ministry/Department/Organisation for specific action needed for meeting the crisis situation.

Crisis Management Group: The Central Relief Commissioner in the Ministry of Home Affairs is the Chairman of the CMG, consisting of senior officers (called nodal officers) from various concerned Ministries. The CMG's functions are to review every year contingency plans formulated by various Ministries/Departments/Organisations in their respective sectors, measures required for dealing with a natural disasters, coordinate the activities of the Central Ministries and the State Governments in relation to disaster preparedness and relief and to obtain information from the nodal officers on measures relating to above.

The CMG, in the event of a natural disaster, meets frequently to review the relief operations and extend all possible assistance required by the affected States to overcome the situation effectively.

The Resident Commissioner of the affected State is also associated with such meetings.

Control Room (Emergency Operation Room): An Emergency Operations Center (Control Room) exists in the nodal Ministry of Home Affairs, which functions round the clock, to assist the Central Relief Commissioner in the discharge of his duties. The activities of the Control Room include collection and transmission of information concerning natural calamity and relief, keeping close contact with governments of the affected States, interaction with other Central Ministries/Departments/Organisations in connection with relief, maintaining records containing all relevant information relating to action points and contact points in Central Ministries etc., keeping up-to-date details of all concerned officers at the Central and State levels.

Contingency Action Plan: A National Contingency Action Plan (CAP) for dealing with contingencies arising in the wake of natural disasters has been formulated by the Government of India and it had been periodically updated. It facilitates the launching of relief operations without delay. The CAP identifies the initiatives required to be taken by various Central Ministries/Departments in the wake of natural calamities, sets down the procedure and determines the focal points in the administrative machinery.

State Relief Manuals: Each State Government has relief manuals/codes which identify that role of each officer in the State for managing the natural disasters. These are reviewed and updated periodically based on the experience of managing the disasters and the need of the State.

Funding mechanisms: The policy and the funding mechanism for provision of relief assistance to those affected by natural calamities is clearly laid down. These are reviewed by the Finance Commission appointed by the Government of India every five years. The Finance Commission makes recommendation regarding the division of tax and non-tax revenues between the Central and the State Governments and also regarding policy for provision of relief assistance and their share of expenditure there on.

A Calamity Relief Fund (CRF) has been set up in each State as per the recommendations of the Eleventh Finance Commission. The size of the Calamity Relief Fund has been fixed by the Finance Commission after taking into account the expenditure on relief and rehabilitation over the past 10 years. The Government of India contributes 75% of the corpus of the Calamity Relief Fund in each State. 25% is contributed to by the State.

Relief assistance to those affected by natural calamities is granted from the CRF. Overall norms for relief assistance are laid down by a national committee with representatives of States as members. Different States can have State specific norms to be recommended by State level committee under the Chief Secretary. Where the calamity is of such proportion that the funds available in the CRF will not be sufficient for provision of relief, the State seeks assistance from the National Calamity Contingency Fund (NCCF)-a fund created at the Central Government level. When such requests are received, the requirements are assessed by a team from the Central Government and thereafter the assessed requirements are cleared by a High Level Committee chaired by the Deputy Prime Minister. In brief, the institutional arrangements for response and relief are wellestablished and have proved to be robust and effective.

In the federal set up of India, the basic responsibility for undertaking rescue, relief and rehabilitation measures in the event of a disaster is that of the State Government concerned. At the State level, response, relief and rehabilitation are handled by Departments of Relief & Rehabilitation. The State Crisis Management Committee set up under the Chairmanship of Chief Secretary who is the highest executive functionary in the State. All the concerned Departments and organisations of the State and Central Government Departments located in the State are represented in this Committee. This Committee reviews the action taken for response and relief and gives guidelines/directions as necessary.

A control room is established under the Relief Commissioner. The control room is in constant touch with the climate monitoring/forecasting agencies and monitors the action being taken by various agencies in performing their responsibilities. The district level is the key level for disaster management and relief activities.

The Collector/Dy. Commissioner is the chief administrator in the district. He is the focal point in the preparation of district plans and in directing, supervising and monitoring calamities for relief. A District Level Coordination and Relief Committee is constituted and is headed by the Collector as Chairman with participation of all other related government and non governmental agencies and departments in addition to the elected representatives.

The Collector is required to maintain close liaison with the district and the State Governments as well as the nearest units of Armed Forces/Central police organisations and other relevant Central Government organisations like Ministries of Communications, Water Resources, Drinking Water, Surface Transport, who could supplement the efforts of the district administration in the rescue and relief operations. The efforts of the Government and non-governmental organisations for response and relief and coordinated by the Collector/Dy. Commissioner.

The District Magistrate/Collector and Coordination Committee under him reviews preparedness measures prior to a impending hazard and coordinate response when the hazard strikes. As all the Departments of the State Government and district level report to the Collector, there is an effective coordination mechanism ensuring holistic response.

New institutional mechanisms: As has been made clear above, the existing mechanisms had based on post-disaster relief and rehabilitation and they have proved to be robust and effective mechanisms in addressing these requirements. The changed policy/approach, however, mandates a priority to full disaster aspects of mitigation, prevention and preparedness and new institutional and policy mechanisms are being put in place to address the policy change. It is proposed to constitute a National Emergency Management Authority at the National level.

The High Powered Committee on Disaster Management which was set up in August, 1999 and submitted its Report in October, 2001, had inter alia recommended that a separate Department of Disaster Management be set up in the Government of India. It was, however, felt that conventional Ministries/Departments have the drawback of not being flexible enough specially in terms of the sanction procedures. The organisation at the Apex level will have to be multi-disciplinary with experts covering a large number of branches.

The National Emergency Management Authority has, therefore, been proposed as a combined Secretariat/Directorate structure-a structure which will be an integral part of the Government and, therefore, will work with the full authority of the Government while, at the same time, retaining the flexibility of a field organisation. The National Emergency Management Authority will be headed by an officer of the rank of Secretary/Special Secretary to the Government in the Ministry of Home Affairs with Special Secretaries/Additional Secretaries from the Ministries/Departments of Health, Water Resources, Environment & Forests, Agriculture, Railways, Atomic Energy, Defence, Chemicals, Science & Technology, Telecommunications, Urban Employment and Poverty Alleviation, Rural Development and India Meteorological Department as Members of the Authority.

The National Emergency Management Authority will have a core permanent secretariat with three divisions-one for Disaster Prevention, Mitigation & Rehabilitation, the other for Preparedness and the third for Human Resource Development. At the State level, as indicated in para-disaster management was being handled by the Departments of Relief & Rehabilitation. As the name suggests, the focus was almost entirely on post-calamity relief. The Government of India is working with the State Governments to convert the Departments of Relief & Rehabilitation into Departments of Disaster Management with an enhanced area of responsibility to include mitigation and preparedness apart from their present responsibilities of relief and rehabilitation.

The changeover has already happened in eight State Governments/Union Territory Administrations. The change is under process in other States. The States have also been asked to set up Disaster Management Authorities under the Chief Minister with Ministers of relevant Departments as members. The objective of setting up an Authority is to ensure that mitigation and preparedness is seen as the joint responsibility of all the Departments concerned and disaster management concerns are mainstreamed into their programmes. This holistic and multidisciplinary approach is the key to effective mitigation.

At the district level, the District Magistrate who is the chief coordinator will be the focal point for coordinating all activities relating to prevention, mitigation and preparedness apart from his existing responsibilities pertaining to response and relief. The District Coordination and Relief Committee is being reconstituted/ re-designated into Disaster Management Committees with officers from relevant departments being added as members. Because of its enhanced mandate of mitigation and prevention, the district heads and departments engaged in development will now be added to the Committee so that mitigation and prevention is mainstreamed into the district plan.

The existing system of drawing up preparedness and response plans will continue. There will, however, also be a long term mitigation plan. District Disaster Management Committees have already been constituted in several districts and are in the process of being constituted in the remaining multi-hazard prone districts. Similarly, we are in the process of creating Block/Taluq Disaster Management Committees in these 169 multi-hazard prone districts in 17 States.

A large number of village level Disaster Management Committees and Disaster Management Teams have already been constituted. The States have been advised to enact Disaster Management Acts. These Acts provide for adequate powers for authorities coordinating mitigation, preparedness and response as well as for mitigation/prevention measures required to be undertaken. Two States, Gujarat & Madhya Pradesh, have already enacted such a law. Other States are in the process. The State Governments have also been advised to convert their Relief Codes into Disaster Management Codes by including aspects of prevention, mitigation and preparedness.

In order to further institutionalise the new approach, the Government of India have decided to enunciate a National Policy on Disaster Management. A draft policy has accordingly been formulated and is expected to be put in place shortly. The policy shall inform all spheres of Central Government activity and shall take precedence over all existing sectoral policies. The broad objectives of the policy are to minimise the loss of lives and social, private and community assets because of natural or manmade disasters and contribute to sustainable development and better standards of living for all, more specifically for the poor and vulnerable sections by ensuring that the development gains are not lost through natural calamities/disasters.

The policy notes that State Governments are primarily responsible for disaster management including prevention and mitigation, while the Government of India provides assistance where necessary as per the norms laid down from time to time and proposes that this overall framework may continue. However, since response to a disaster requires coordination of resources available across all the Departments of the Government, the policy mandates that the Central Government will, in conjunction with the State Governments, seek to ensure that such a coordination mechanism is laid down through an appropriate chain of command so that mobilisation of resources is facilitated.

7.3. Early Warning System

7.3.1. Cyclone Warning

Tropical Cyclones are intense low pressure systems which develop over warm sea. They are capable of causing immense damage due to strong winds, heavy rains and storm surges. The frequency of the TC in the Bay of Bengal is 4 to 5 times more than in the Arabian Sea. About 35% of initial disturbances in the north Indian ocean reach TC stage of which 45% become severe.

Indian Meteorological Department (IMD) is mandated to monitor and give warnings regarding Tropical Cyclone (TC). Monitoring process has been revolutionised by the advent of remote sensing techniques. A TC intensity analysis and forecast scheme has been worked out using satellite image interpretation techniques which facilitate forecasting of storm surges. Data resources are crucial to early forecasting of cyclones. Satellite based observations are being extensively utilised.

Satellite integrated automated weather stations have been installed on islands, oilrigs and exposed coastal sites. Buoys for supplementing the surface data network in the tropical ocean have been deployed. The Government have also started a National Data Buoy Programme. A set of 12 moored buoys have been deployed in the northern Indian Ocean to provide meteorological and oceanographic data.

Dynamic forecasting of TCs requires knowledge of the vertical structure of both the Cyclone and the surrounding environment. The rawin sonde remains the principal equipment for sounding. The Doppler Radar wind profiler provides hourly soundings. A mesosphere, stratosphere, troposphere (MST) radar has also been installed at Thirupatti. Another profiler is being developed and will be deployed at IMD Pune. Another important source of upper level data is the aircraft reports.

Increasing number of commercial jet aircraft are equipped with the Aircraft Meteorological Data Relay system. This data is being made available is also being used by the IMD for analysis and predictions. Radars have been used to observe TCs since long. Surveillance of the spiral rain bands and the eye of the TC is an important function of the coastal radars. Ten Cyclones Detection Radars have already been installed. These radars are providing useful estimates of storm centres upto a range 300-400 Km. Doppler radars provide direct measurements of wind fields in TCs.

Due to range limitation, Doppler wind estimates are usually within a range of about 100 Km. IMD has deployed Doppler radars at 3 sites on the east coast. Another set of 3 Doppler radars are being deployed in Andhra Pradesh in near future. The meteorological satellite has made a tremendous impact on the analysis of cyclones. All developing cloud clusters are routinely observed through satellite cloud imagery & those showing signs of organisation are closely monitored for signs of intensification.

The goal of any warning system is to maximise the number of people who take appropriate and timely action for the safety of life and property. All warning systems start with detection of the event and with people getting out of harm's way. Such warning systems encompass three equally important elements namely; Detection and Warning; Communication; and Response. The two stage warning system has been in existence since long in IMD. Recently it has been improved upon by introducing two more stages-the 'Pre-Cyclone watch' and the 'post-landfall Scenario'. This four stage warning system meets the requirements of Public Administrators and Crisis Managers.

The 'Pre-Cyclone Watch' stage, contains early warning about the development of a cyclonic disturbance in the form of monsoon depression which has a potential to threaten the coast with cyclone force winds. The coastal stretch likely to be affected is identified. This early warning bulletin is issued by the IMD before the Cyclone-Alert Stage. This provides enough lead time for the crisis managers to undertake preparedness actions.

After the early warning on the 'Pre-Cyclone Watch' the Collectors of coastal and few immediate interior districts and the Chief Secretary of the concerned maritime State are warned in two stages, whenever any coastal belt is expected to experience adverse weather (heavy rain/gales/tidal wave) in association with a cyclonic storm or a depression likely to intensify into a cyclonic storm.

The second stage of "Cyclone Alert" is sounded 48 hours in advance of the expected commencement of adverse weather over the coastal areas. Forecasts of commencement of strong winds, heavy precipitation along the coast in association with arrival of cyclone are issued at the alert stage. Landfall point is usually not identified at this stage. The third stage warning known as "Cyclone Warning" is issued 24 hours in advance. Landfall point is forecast in this stage of cyclone warning.

In addition to the forecasts for heavy rains and strong winds, the storm surge forecast is also issued. Since the storm surge is the biggest killer so far as the devastating attributes of a storm are concerned, information in this regard is most critical for taking follow up action for evacuation from the low lying areas likely to be affected by the storm. After the landfall of the cyclone the strong winds with gale force speeds continue over certain interior districts of the maritime States hit by the cyclone.

To take cognisance of that, a fourth stage known as 'Post-landfall Scenario Stage' is now identified usually as a part of the 'Cyclone Warning Stage' either at the time of landfall of the disturbance or about twelve hour in advance of it. It includes warnings of strong winds and heavy rains likely to be encountered in the interior districts. For communications, the IMD makes use of 97 point-to-point teleprinter links connecting different field offices.

7.3.2. Flood Warning System

Flooding is caused by the inadequate capacity within the banks of the rivers to contain the high flow brought down from the upper catchments due to heavy rainfall. It is also caused by accumulation of water resulting from heavy spells of rainfall over areas, which have got poor drainage characteristics.

Flooding is accentuated by erosion and silting leading to meandering of the rivers in plains and reduction in carrying capacity of the river channel. It is also aggravated by earthquakes and land slides, leading to changes in river course and obstructions to flow. Synchronisation of floods in the main rivers and tributaries and retardation of flow due to tidal effects lead to major floods.

Cyclones bring in their wake considerable loss of life and property. The flood forecasting and warning system is used for alerting the likely damage centers well in advance of the actual arrival of floods, to enable the people to move and also to remove the moveable property to safer places or to raised platforms specially constructed for the purpose. A beginning in scientific flood forecasting was made in November, 1958 by Central Water Commission when a Flood Forecasting Centre was set up at its Headquarters, at Delhi, for giving timely Forecasts and Warnings of the incoming floods to the villages located in the river areas around the National Capital, Delhi.

A computerised monitoring system has been developed under which daily water levels as observed at 0800 hrs and forecasts issued by field units are transmitted to CWC headquarters in New Delhi. Based on the compilation of all such data received from field divisions, daily water level and flood forecast bulletins in two parts for stage and for inflow forecasting stations respectively. Special Yellow Bulletins are issued whenever the river stage at the forecasting site attains a level within 0.50 m of its previous HFL. Red Bulletins highlighting security of the problem are also issued whenever the water level at the forecasting stations equals or exceeds previous HFL.

7.4. Prevention of Disaster

The Government of India have adopted mitigation and prevention as essential components of their development strategy. The Tenth Five Year Plan emphasises the fact that development cannot be sustainable without mitigation being built into developmental process. Each State is supposed to prepare a plan scheme for disaster mitigation in accordance with the approach outlined in the plan. In brief, mitigation is being institutionalised into developmental planning.

The Finance Commission makes recommendations with regard to devolution of funds between the Central Government and State Governments as also outlays for relief and rehabilitation. The earlier Finance Commissions were mandated to look at relief and rehabilitation. The Terms of Reference of the Twelfth Finance Commission have been changed and the Finance Commission has been mandated to look at the requirements for mitigation and prevention apart from its existing mandate of looking at relief and rehabilitation. A Memorandum has been submitted to the Twelfth Finance Commission after consultation with States. The Memorandum proposes a Mitigation Fund.

The Government of India have issued guidelines that where there is a shelf of projects, projects addressing mitigation will be given a priority. It has also been mandated that each project in a hazard prone area will have disaster prevention/mitigation as a term of reference and the project document has to reflect as to how the project addresses that term of reference. Measures for flood mitigation were taken from 1950 onwards. As against the total of 40 million hectares prone to floods, area of about 15 million hectares have been protected by construction of embankments.

A number of dams and barrages have been constructed. The State Governments have been assisted to take up mitigation programmes like construction of raised platforms etc. Floods continue to be a menace however mainly because of the huge quantum of silt being carried by the rivers emanating from the Himalayas. This silt has raised the bed level in many rivers to above the level of the countryside. Embankments have also gives rise to problems of drainage with heavy rainfall leading to water logging in areas outside the embankment.

Due to erratic behaviour of monsoons, both low and medium rain fall regions, which constitute about 68% of the total area, are vulnerable to periodical droughts. Our experience has been that almost every third year is a drought year. However, in some of the States, there may be successive drought years enhancing the vulnerability of the population in these areas. Local communities have devised indigenous safety mechanisms and drought oriented farming methods in many parts of the country.

In the rural areas, the bulk of the housing is non-engineered construction. The mode of construction in the rural areas has also changed from mud and thatch to brick and concrete construction thereby increasing the vulnerability. The increasing population has led to settlements in vulnerable areas close to the river bed areas which are prone to liquefaction. The Government have moved to address these issues.

A National Core Group for Earthquake Mitigation has been constituted consisting of experts in earthquake engineering and administrators. The Core Group has been assigned with the responsibility of drawing up a strategy and plan of action for mitigating the impact of earthquakes; providing advice and guidance to the States on various aspects of earthquake mitigation; developing/organising the preparation of handbooks/pamphlets/ type designs for earthquake resistant construction; working out systems for assisting the States in the seismically vulnerable zones to adopt/integrate appropriate Bureau of Indian Standards codes in their building bye-laws; evolving systems for training of municipal engineers as also practicing architects and engineers in the private sector in the salient features of Bureau of Indian Standards codes and the amended bye-laws; evolving a system of certification of architects/engineers for testing their knowledge of earthquake resistant construction; evolving systems for training of masons and carry out intensive awareness generation campaigns.

An earthquake mitigation project has been finalised for reducing the vulnerability to earthquakes. The programme includes detailed evaluation and retrofitting of lifeline buildings such as hospitals, schools, water and power supply units, telecommunication buildings, airports/airport control towers, railway stations, bus stands and important administrative buildings. The programme also includes training of more than one hundred thousand masons for earthquake resistant constructions. Besides, assistance will be provided under this project to the State Governments to put in place appropriate techno legal regime.

An accelerated urban earthquake vulnerability reduction programme has been taken up in 38 cities in seismic zones III, IV & V with population of half a million and above. Sensitisation workshop for engineers/architects, government functionaries and voluntary organisations have already been held in 36 of the 38 cities.

Disaster mitigation and preparedness plans are under preparation in these cities. Awareness generation campaign has already been undertaken. The orientation courses for engineers and architects have been organised to impart knowledge about seismically safe construction and implementation of BIS norms. This programme will be further extended to 166 earthquake prone districts in seismic zones IV & V.

Rural housing and community assets for vulnerable sections of the population are created at a fairly large scale by the Ministry of Rural Development under the Indira Awas Yojna (IAY) and Sampooran Grameen Rojgar Yojna (SGRY). About 250 thousand small but compact units are constructed every year, besides community assets such as community centres, recreation centres, anganwadi centres etc. Technology support is provided by about two hundred rural housing centres spread over the entire country.

The Ministry of Rural Development are now under the process of revising their guidelines for construction of such dwelling units by incorporating appropriate earthquake/cyclone resistant features. Training to the functionaries in the rural housing centres will be organised through the Ministry of Home Affairs. This initiative is expected to go a long way for the construction and popularisation of seismically safe construction at village/block level.

The cyclone shelters will be multi purpose units to be run as schools or community centres in normal times and will have capacity to house 3000 to 5000 persons with adequate number of toilets, community kitchen and other facilities. Areas will be identified for providing shelter to livestock. In the engineering designs for construction, special attention will be paid to the attachment of roof to the dwelling units so as to make such units cyclone proof, besides incorporating earthquake resistant features. The project will be taken up shortly and is expected to be completed over a period of five years.

A Disaster Risk Management Programme has been taken up with the assistance from UNDP, USAID and European Union in 169 most hazard prone districts in 17 States including all the 8 North Eastern State. The implementation of the project commenced from October, 2002 and is expected to be concluded by December, 2007. The programme components include awareness generation and public education, preparedness, planning and capacity building, developing appropriate policies, institutional, administrative, legal and techno-legal regime at State, District, Block, village, urban local body and ward levels for vulnerability reduction. Under this programme Disaster Management Plans have been prepared for about 3500 villages, 250 Gram Panchayat, 60 blocks and 15 districts.

Elected representatives of over 8000 Panchayati Raj Institutions have already been trained, besides imparting training to Members of voluntary organisations. Training is being imparted to master trainers under the programme. More than 600 master trainers and 1000 teachers have already been trained in different districts in disaster mitigation.

Disaster Management Committees consisting of elected representatives, civil society members, Civil Defence volunteers and Government functionaries have been constituted at all levels including village/urban local body/ward levels. Disaster Management Teams have been constituted in villages and are being imparted training in basic functions of first aid, rescue, evacuation and related issues. The thrust of the programme is to build up capabilities of the community since the community is invariably the first responder.

The National Centre for Disaster Management at the national level has been upgraded and designated as the National Institute of Disaster Management. It is being developed as a Regional Centre of Excellence in Asia. The National Institute of Disaster Management will develop training modules at different levels, undertake training of trainers and organise training programmes for planners, administrators and command functionaries. Besides, the other functions assigned to the National Institute of Disaster Management include development of exhaustive National level information base on disaster management policies, prevention mechanisms, mitigation measures; formulation of disaster management code and providing consultancy to various States in strengthening their disaster management systems and capacities as well as preparation of disaster management plans and strategies for hazard mitigation and disaster response.

Disaster Management faculties have already been created in 29 State level training institutes located in 28 States. These faculties are being directly supported by the Ministry of Home Affairs. The State Training Institutions take up several focused training programmes for different target groups within the State. The Disaster Management faculties in these Institutes are being further strengthened so as to enable them to develop as Institutes of Excellence for a specific disaster. This system has already been institutionalised and is being further strengthened so as to make it a focal point in each State for development of human resources in disaster mitigation and preparedness.

7.5. Mitigation and Preparedness

Mitigation and preparedness measures go hand in hand for vulnerability reduction and rapid professional response to disasters. The Bhuj earthquake in January, 2001 brought out several inadequacies in the system. The search and rescue teams had not been trained professionally; specialised dog squad to look for live bodies under the debris were not available; and there was no centralised resource inventory for emergency response. Although army played a pivotal role in search and rescue and also set up their hospital after the collapse of Government hospital at Bhuj, the need for fully equipped mobile hospitals with trained personnel was felt acutely.

Despite these constraints, the response was fairly well organised. However, had these constraints been taken care of before hand, the response would have been even more professional and rapid which may have reduced the loss of lives. Specialist search and rescue teams from other countries did reach Bhuj. However, precious time was lost and even with these specialist teams it was not possible to cover all severely affected areas as quickly as the Government would have desired. It was, therefore, decided that we should remove these inadequacies and be in a stage of preparedness at all times.

Pending arrival of the specialist teams, the battalions located near the site of incident would be deployed immediately. For this purpose, a curriculum has been drawn up and integrated into the training curriculum of CPMFs. The States have also been advised to set up their own specialist teams for responding to disasters. Assistance will be provided to the State Governments for training their trainers at the national institutes already designated for this purpose. The State Governments' search and rescue teams to be constituted from the State Police will be equipped to meet the requirement. For this purpose, the State Governments have been authorised to utilise 10% of the annual allocation made under the Contingency Relief Fund for purchase of equipments.

Fourteen Regional Response Centres are being set up in different parts of the country. These centres will have response teams and equipment and resources for being able to response to any hazard/calamity in the neighbouring States. A Steering Committee has been constituted in the Ministry to oversee the creation of capabilities for emergency response. A 200 bedded mobile hospital, fully trained and equipped is being set up by the Ministry of Health and attached to a leading Government hospital in Delhi.

Three additional mobile hospitals with all medical and emergency equipments are proposed to be located in different parts of the country. These mobile hospitals will also be attached to the leading Government hospitals in the country. This will enable the mobile hospitals to extend assistance to the hospitals with which they are attached in normal time. They will be airlifted during emergencies with additional doctors/paramedics taken from the hospitals with which the mobile hospitals are attached to the site of disaster. It is proposed to purchase dedicated aircraft and helicopters with a view to reducing the response time.

The issue is pending for consideration and approval of Empowered Group of Ministers on Disaster Management. Once the airlift facilities are developed for exclusive use for disaster management, it will be possible to provide airlift facilities to specialist search and rescue teams, mobile hospitals and equipments. In order to professionalise the response, it is proposed to introduce the Incident Command System in the country. This system provides for specialist incident command teams with an Incident Commander and officers trained in different aspects of incident management-logistics, operations, planning, safety, media management etc.

Communication is a major bottleneck in case of any major disaster particularly when the traditional network system already in force brake down. In order to strengthen communications, it has been decided that police network (POLNET) will also be used for disaster management. For this purpose POLNET communication facility will be extended to District Magistrates, Sub Divisional Magistrates as well as the Control Rooms. For emergency communication, mobile satellite based units which can be transported to the site of the disaster are being procured.

The GIS data base already available with different agencies of the Government is being upgraded and the gaps are proposed to be bridged. A project for this purpose is being drawn up with a view to institutionalising the arrangements. The data base will provide multi layered maps on district wise basis. Three maps taken in conjunction with the satellite images available for a particular area will enable the district administration as well as State Governments to carry out hazard zonation and vulnerability assessment, as well as coordinate response after a disaster.

In order to further strengthen the capacity for response, the fire services are proposed to be developed into multi hazard response units as is the normal practice in several other countries. It is proposed to provide rescue tenders in addition to fire tenders to each fire unit and fill up all gaps upto sub-divisional level. Hazmat vans will be provided to State capitals and metropolitan cities. This will necessitate recruitment of additional fire men and drivers and intensive training required to be provided to enable them to function as efficient of all purpose response units.

A project for development of fire service into all hazard response units has also been finalised and submitted for obtaining necessary financial approval. India has a large network of Civil Defence and Home Guards volunteers. The existing strength is about 1.2 million. However, this organisation has not so far been associated with disaster mitigation, preparedness and response functions. It is proposed to revamp the Civil Defence organisation to enable them to discharge a key responsibility in all the facets of disaster management including preparedness. A proposal in this regard has been finalised and is under consideration of the Government.

Standard Operating Procedures are being laid down to ensure all the steps required to be taken for disaster management are put in place. The Standard Operating Procedure will also in encompass response, besides preparedness. With the development of disaster management committees and disaster management teams at all levels including village/urban local body/ward level, the stage will be set for comprehensive preparedness measures to be taken with active participation of the community and non-governmental organisations.

References

Bhatta, Braja Bandhu, *The natural calamities in Orissa in the 19th century*, New Delhi: Commonwealth Publishers, 1997.

Gupta, H.K. (ed.), *Latur earthquake*, Bangalore : Geological Society of India, 1994.

Sharma, Vinod K. (ed.), *Disaster management*, New Delhi: National Centre for Disaster Management, Indian Institute of Public Administration, 2001.

Suryanarayana, M., "Marine fisherfolk of north-east coastal Andhra Pradesh", Calcutta: Anthropological Survey of India, Govt. of India, 1977.

CHAPTER 5

Role of News Media in Disaster Management

Viewing the news media is an institution with a process, provides a helpful framework for reviewing more closely the news information which originates in many forms and is subject to many influences. Before reaching the media, information is handled by a host of stakeholders, many of whom are influenced not by the objective news value of a given event but by political, professional, or commercial motives.

8.1. News Uniformity

Despite multiple interests and influences, the product that emerges form the system bears much uniformity across competing sections of the media. As a foreign news radio editor said, "No one in the media wants to take the chance of being wrong, so they stick to consumers' view of the news." At the same time, while commercial competition may contribute to a certain uniformity in news coverage, different media inject different commercial criteria and, in some cases, political considerations that affect the content and style of coverage. Since the product is available to policy elites and public alike, the media is regarded by some observers as a lowest common denominator within which multiple actors in a crisis find themselves reduced to a common field of arbitration.

8.1.1. Types of News Media

In practice, news information comes to the consumer at different speeds, in various packages, with different shelf lives. For the purposes of this analysis, three broad types of news coverage are identified.

Headline news: Television and radio news bulletins as well as news summary sections of print media constitute what might be called headline news. The emphasis is on reporting the latest developments in fast-moving or breaking stories and scooping the opposition rather than on presenting an in-depth analysis of events.

Documentary news: Documentary news, which enjoys a longer shelf life, may offer more detailed background and analysis of an issue, demonstrating the investigative or analytical skills of a particular news outlet or reporter. This kind of coverage is typically found in specialist broadcast features and on inside pages of newspapers and journals. Some newspapers have little space for documentary news and, give preference to local or national rather than international topics.

News commentary: A third category, news commentary, is represented by editorials or opinion pieces that carry a particular point of view on the issues of the moment. Such commentaries are an extension of policy processes, often used by governments and policy elites to make their own views known. Use by nongovernmental commentators also demonstrates the autonomy of news organisations and represents an obvious source of media impact on policy. News commentary provides perhaps the most obvious vehicle through which publishers and editors can communicate their institutional or personal viewpoints.

These three broad types of news information are not mutually exclusive, but overlap and interact. All three affect the formation of public policy and the shape of humanitarian action. Policymakers and aid groups often overlook how much modern news information is tailored to different audiences, with different style and content.

8.1.2. Structure and Trends

Electronic and print media: Within the news industry, a broad division exists between electronic and print media. Each has maintained a separate niche in the commercial and news markets while using the other as a source. Television and radio journalists regularly scan newspapers and journals for story ideas; the print media often utilise their greater capacity to follow up headline news items in more depth. Many journalists - and some policymakers as well - admit to using CNN as a kind of wire service for monitoring fast-breaking stories. Changing technology, in particular the development of electronic newspapers and interactive television, may blur the remaining distinctions between electronic and print media and rearrange the gatekeepers in the system.

Television news: Much of the post-Cold War debate about media influence on foreign policy has focused on television as the most potent actor. Drawing upon satellite technology, television news bulletins depict the violence and suffering of conflicts with an immediacy and realism that, some argue, forces a rapid policy response.

Market audience: The media also need to be differentiated according to their basic market audience of readership. Although they have access to a global pool of pictures and to far-flung reporting, the majority of media are still national in focus. So, too, is the content of most news programs and publications. Even services such as CNN or ITN World News, that are marketed as global, invariably reflect U.S. and British domestic perspectives and values. Commercial demands also have blurred the traditional division of news media into those serving "quality" as distinct from "tabloid" markets. Electronic and print media are now finely tuned to link audiences or readership with advertisers. Increasingly, the media have to resort to packaging news in a new form of tabloidism that mixes information with entertainment. Judging form the reception, the resulting blend dubbed "infotainment" is both profitable from a commercial standpoint and questionable from a journalistic one.

Several international media organisations stand out as noteworthy exceptions to these trends. These include the BBC World Service radio and the International Herald-Tribune newspaper, which maintain high standards of comprehensive reporting and are regarded as sources of authenticity in international affairs. This is not to say that such media are necessarily influential in the highest levels of policy processes. As a British government policymaker noted, only a limited number of broadcast institutions such as BBC Radio News and ITN bulletins exercise serious influence on senior officials and politicians.

8.2. Journalistic Ethics

The news media in general and journalists in particular are wary of suggestions that they have, or should adopt, a humanitarian agenda. The majority of professional journalists pride themselves on the "journalistic ethic" which dictates that they report the news in an objective and "morally neutral" fashion. Since their primary mission is not humanitarian, international and humanitarian matters must compete for attention with business, sports, entertainment, domestic politics, and other news. The proposition that the media give special attention to humanitarian issues is similar to requests by other special interests for expanded coverage of activities in which they are involved and is viewed as a flagrant violation of journalistic ethics.

8.2.1. Humanitarian Interests and Instincts

While different independent news sources and journalists may agree on the need to preserve the journalistic ethic, they vary in their interests and the relative emphasis, which they place on covering international and humanitarian issues. The humanitarian instincts and personal objectives of working journalists can also affect the way a given news institution functions. Some journalists carry a strong personal humanitarian agenda, take great personal risks in reporting conflicts and suffering, and are committed to seeing that their work contributes to a more-effective global response.

In conflict after conflict, journalists strike up not only working relationships but also friendships with humanitarian personnel. While they must work to preserve their objectivity as reporters, the fact that they take more than a professional interest in the issues is undeniable. Their reporting helps establish, and builds on, a palpable human interest among news consumers.

8.3. News Media During Crisis

Another major factor in determining media coverage is the net news value of a particular crisis. A glance at daily headlines and bulletins in competing markets demonstrates a striking consistency. Attempts to determine whether that consistency reflects an intrinsic objectivity in news coverage or, more negatively, the uniform currency created by the demands of competition have confronted analysts with a maze of contradictory data. Research and conventional wisdom, however, suggest that the value of a particular crisis is deliberately or intuitively subject to a number of filters or criteria which, determines its "news value" relative to competing stories.

8.3.1. Limitations of News Media

Analysts of how the media function in complex emergencies note limitations in the sufficiency and adequacy of coverage provided. Many factors and trends contribute to these limitations.

8.3.1.1. Reduced foreign coverage

Fires, the amount of news coverage of complex emergencies is widely held to be insufficient. The number of major crises in which there is widespread and serious human deprivation and abuse of human rights outruns the coverage provided. At precisely the time when major crises have proliferated, many news organisations have reduced the space devoted to these events. That situation seems unlikely to change as commercial pressures continue to force a reduction in foreign news-gathering operations.

8.3.1.2. Focusing on breaking events

The media have been criticised for providing too much attention to breaking events and too little historical and political context. A notable example is the reporting of the Rwanda crisis. During the initial phase, when a pre-planned campaign of genocide took place, international coverage was insufficient, with only a handful of reporters on the scene. Later, however, when hundreds of reporters chronicled the distress of Rwandan refugees in neighbouring countries, coverage was inadequate. Few journalists noted that the population in refugee camps was composed of Rwandan communities transported largely intact, including political and military elements implicated in the genocide.

8.3.1.3. Focusing on the sensational and exceptional

The news media as well as the government policymakers and humanitarian institutions, missed clear early warning signs in Somalia of the deteriorating situation and obvious forerunners in Burundi for what was to follow in Rwanda. The limitations of headline news in these various cases might suggest documentary coverage as a more likely early warning agent.

8.3.1.4. Judging news value

Another major area of criticism is that the international media have focused on subjects of perceived interest to readers and viewers in developed countries. These include the threats posed by a given crisis to Western values and the activities of expatriate-generally North American and European-aid workers and the involvement of Western troops. The presence of international military forces invariably ensures coverage and provides the focus for the media of the troop-sending nation.

Foreign news is often given highly subjective treatment by media committed to serving domestic markets. As a result, foreign conflicts carrying no obvious or immediate threat may be presented in the Western media only when they are advanced well beyond the stage of prevention or containment. Even active conflicts are not assured coverage.

8.3.1.5. Perpetuating negative images

A related criticism concerns the perceived tendency of the media to perpetuate negative images and ethnocentric views. Persons affected by international crises often are portrayed as helpless victims who are dependent on, and take liberties with, international largesse. The fact that those who suffer are often nonwhite and their "rescuers" white has contributed to charges of racism in news coverage. Critics also speak of the "pornography of suffering," that is, of the dehumanisation in the portrayal of those who suffer. On occasion, the beneficiaries of assistance have criticised the media and humanitarian institutions for the images conveyed.

8.3.1.6. Belittling complex situations

Complex situations in war zones are frequently reduced to infotainment rather than treated in news documentary or news commentary format. Often a human-interest angle is identified to emphasise the connection to a domestic audience.

8.3.1.7. Limited coverage areas

The difficulty in gaining access in complex emergencies and the high costs of producing usable footage or reports can be prohibitive. With respect to Rwanda, after months of limited coverage of genocide that claimed between 500,000 and one million lives, the resulting refugee emergency, complete with the specter of cholera, became the top international news story of the day. CNN, which was alerted to the likelihood of the outbreak of genocide in early April, opted against reporting on developments until three months later, when the genocide produced a mass migration of Hutus into neighbouring countries. Increased coverage resulted in part from greater security and accessibility in Goma than in Kigali, and the involvement in the relief effort of many national military contingents and myriad humanitarian organisations.

8.4. Media Influence

Media impact on policy may be identified in two ways: by the level of policy at which impact occurs and by the degree of influence the media exercises. Although the media may influence policy and humanitarian response, other factors, especially domestic political contexts are at least as important in determining governmental responses. Where the media has clear impact, however, television coverage has been critical.

8.4.1. Stages of Response

It is important to distinguish the stage of response crisis at which the interaction of the institutions of the crisis triangle is being assessed. In workshops, which served as the basis for this analysis, participants identified four broad stages, beginning with the "discovery" of a given crisis by the media, sometimes with the help of humanitarian organisations and sometimes government officials. The discovery of a crisis is often followed by "inundation"-the period of snowballing interest as the media, government officials, and humanitarian groups flock to the scene in an effort to be identified with the action.

8.4.2. Stages of Policymaking

Any attempts to measure the effect of the news media on government policy needs first to identify the stage of the policy process at which the effect operates. In this regard, the focus necessarily shifts among different governmental institutions as the crisis appears on different agendas. Perhaps the most detailed illustration of the interaction was provided by growing media coverage of Somalia, traced alongside the incremental ascent of the crisis on the agendas of various government officials in Washington. To the extent that comparable detail is known about other crises, media effects might follow a similar progression.

8.4.3. Impact of Media on Policy

Policymakers can respond to media coverage in one of three broad ways: strategic, tactical or presentational. Simplified for analytical purposes, they nevertheless help to differentiate impacts at the various levels of policy formulation. Particular crises also can move across these levels as their perceived relevance to national interests changes.

Strategic: The media, especially television, may have a noticeable influence on broad matters of government strategy. These include decisions on whether or not to intervene in a crisis, whether to change radically the nature of a given intervention, or whether to withdraw altogether.

Tactical: At the more operational or tactical level, the news media may have a significant influence, whether or not they have played a role in the shape of the overall strategy. In Bosnia, for example, increased measured to protect Sarajevo-no-fly zones, weapons collection points, and aerial attacks-were tactical innovations that responded in part to media coverage and growing public concern. These measures became the focus of extensive media coverage, but they never challenged the overall Western strategy of avoiding a more confrontational and forcible approach.

Presentational: The media may stimulate cosmetic changes in policy that are designed primarily for media presentation and public consumption. In this category are such actions as medical evacuations by the British government of a small number of victims from Bosnia and the limited humanitarian response by the U.S. military in Rwanda. These kinds of action also may represent tactical responses to a given problem, but they are "presentational" in that, however constructive in their own right, they probably would not have been undertaken apart from the media exposure that accompanied them. Such measures amount to little more than photo opportunities that create difficulties in distinguishing reality from the presented image.

The degrees of influence described are based on the collective judgments of participants and observers, although there is little unanimity among them. The media dominate, control or even supplant the usual policy processes, sidelining the normal institutions of policymaking.

8.4.3.1. Effects of media on humanitarian Responses

Governmental response to humanitarian crises has clearly changed during the early post-Cold War period. Initial willingness by governments to respond more actively, first with the intervention in northern Iraq and then Somalia, as been followed by greater caution in Bosnia and Rwanda. Early experience may well have alerted policymakers to the dangers of overreaction to the media. Media effect on policy has become more limited, often liked to humanitarian as distinct from political or military action

Humanitarian action is likely to proceed on a case-by-case basis, with consistent principles and practice still a matter of discussion.

8.4.3.2. Effect of media within war zones

The effect of the media in complex emergencies and the roles of external and local media are increasingly recognised as key factors in the generation, continuation, and resolution of humanitarian crises. Since each acts in different political contexts, the use of the media as a tool of diplomacy or propaganda is of particular concern. The policy impacts of external media are normally played out in far-off capitals, but they also can have a significant impact on in-country operations. The case studies in the next chapter demonstrate that the external media can act as humanitarian agents, encouraging the targeting of aid toward areas of publicised need or discouraging human rights violations.

The media native to conflict areas - be they local, national, or regional-are a potential force for reconciliation in civil war settings. They also may be used by humanitarian agencies to ensure greater transparency of operations. Frequently, with a focus on influencing governments and publics in donor countries, expatriates in war zones concentrate media relations efforts on Western news organisations to the exclusion of indigenous channels, but for indigenous outlets to achieve their full potential, international actors need explicit strategies that nurture working relationships with them. Local media often reflect and deepen the politicisation of conflicts as the former Yugoslavia and Rwanda demonstrate. Though external media can become targets of manipulation by warring factions, where local media are thoroughly politicised, external media carry a heavier burden of responsibility to convey accurate information and to encourage reconciliation.

8.4.3.3. Effect of the media on humanitarian action

The media have an impact on humanitarian action in high-profile crises: that impact appears to be greater than the impact of humanitarian actors on the media. The imbalance reflects a variety of factors, including the lack of coordination among humanitarian groups and the lack of individual and corporate strategies for relating to the media as an institution. Humanitarian agencies enjoy a privileged position to influence policy processes, both directly and through the media. Their uneven success rate in doing so in part reflects variables in media-policy interaction that are beyond the control such agencies, and in part results from structural limitations. Coordination among humanitarian organisations is difficult, straddling, as they do, agencies in the intergovernmental, governmental, and nongovernmental arenas, each with divergent points of view. Consensus is lacking on matters such as how to ensure the security of humanitarian operations and how to relate to the increased activism of international military forces in the humanitarian sphere.

The news media can sometimes be implicated in undesirable developments on the humanitarian front. Coverage of the deteriorating situation in Goma helped stimulate an enormous outpouring of resources from governments and the public. Yet it also led to increased posturing and competition among a wide array of aid groups and to the imbalance of resource allocations -to the advantage of photogenic sectors and refugees and to the detriment of Rwanda's own reconstruction agenda and internally displaced persons. The opportunism of humanitarian organisations in these circumstances has led to serious and recurring questions about their professionalism and accountability.

The capacity of the media, using the latest technology, to convey information rapidly is also exerting new pressures on humanitarian actors. Amnesty International members who see atrocities on television demand to know what their organisation is doing to address them. Some personnel fear that such pressure may introduce changes in their organisational cultures. The traditional emphasis on doing what is needed - which often requires patience, nuance, and discretion - could give way to a push to do anything quick and visible. The need o agencies to be perceived as in the vanguard rather than playing catch-up with media-identified crises has negative as well as positive aspects.

Humanitarian actions, whether as a concerted policy or as a substitute for more vigorous diplomacy and military intervention, has enjoyed a high profile. As a short-term measure, humanitarian action offers an effective counter to media pressure on policymakers. But for governments and humanitarian agencies, aid-only response falls short in situations in which insecurity is high and political and diplomatic objectives remain unclear. While honest scrutiny of these failings may weaken short-term support for humanitarian action, it also may contribute over the longer term to the effectiveness of such action.

8.5. Future Policy

Reflecting governmental attitudes, the levels of political will and the resources necessary to combat humanitarian crises are likely to fall far short of demand in the years ahead. The uneven results of international initiatives mounted during the early post-Cold War years probably will contribute to a retrenchment. Yet the actual and potential demand for assistance will grow. Despite the need for clearer criteria for action and greater cost-effectiveness in the activities mounted, the most likely response of the international community for the time being will be to judge and manage each crisis on a case-by-basis. In such a context for reasons examined earlier, there is greater potential for media influence on policy debate and outcomes.

The likely increase in internal armed conflicts during the coming years presents humanitarian agencies with major dilemmas. For example, they stand to win greater backing for their actions to provide emergency assistance as they lose support for the more difficult but ultimately more critical tasks of tackling the root causes of distress and of development education in their own societies. Moreover, as governments lose a taste for security interventions, humanitarian agencies find themselves increasingly in the vanguard of international action, dealing with warring factions that are quickly learning how to manipulate external actors. Media attention to humanitarian activities is also likely to continue its erratic course, with increased or sympathetic coverage by no means guaranteed.

8.5.1. New Technology and Increased Commercialism

The revolution in information technology and the proliferation of news media channels have left commentators divided about future media coverage of foreign affairs. In one assessment, consumers using the new technology are more likely to have access to a greater variety of information sources, allowing them to bypass traditional gatekeepers in the media.

The implications of parallel developments in cyberspace are not yet fully clear. Although the Internet promises an unequaled information system for those involved in humanitarian crises, more information does not necessarily bring greater understanding. The main attraction of the Internet is its anarchy and freedom of access, but this attraction may also become its major drawback. Journalists and editors already have vast information from which to select news. Likewise, policymakers and others with specialised interests will turn to new information services only if they offer faster access to better information. In summary, there is no conclusive evidence yet that the public is turning away from traditional news sources or local preoccupation. Nor is there any assurance that technological progress will result in improved quantity or quality of media coverage of humanitarian concerns.

8.5.2. Responsibilities of the Media

The media have a widely acknowledged responsibility to contribute to the education of domestic audiences about the wider threats of complex emergencies, if not through headline news then through other types of coverage. At the same time, however, they are well advised to retain an independent perspective on humanitarian crises. This will require keeping their distance from the agendas of both governments and humanitarian organisations, each of which is an important source of information, but each of which also has special interests to promote.

The media inevitably will require some time before they are in a position to make their own judgments on the spot in each new crisis, but there is no reason why hard-hitting commentary should wait until the winding down of a relief operation or of media presence. A subject well within the purview of media attention would involve analysis of why major emergencies sometimes recur in the "same setting, and why they occur in settings that have received ample development assistance over a period of years.

The media also have a contribution to make, and a responsibility to make it, in monitoring post-conflict reconstruction, even though policymakers and relief groups may have moved on to the next crisis. Again, the retrospective role is more likely to be covered in documentary news. Exercising accountability will require an ability to make discriminating judgments. Unwarranted criticism - of the strategies of donor governments in dealing with warring parties, of the warring parties themselves, and of humanitarian actors - can represent a setback to effective responses. As with the other two major actors in such conflicts, the media will need to balance its responsibility to "tell it like it is" against its need for access and information.

In addition to exercising accountability in relation to other institutions of the crisis triangle, the media should subject itself to higher standars of accountability. As the activities of governments and humanitarian organisations come under greater scrutiny, so, too, will the effects of the media as a humanitarian actor. Certainly the impact of its activities can be profound. The media in general, and television in particular, are well aware of the power of the picture. Not only do the most dramatic pictures dominate headline news but they also can have an impact on other media.

8.5.3. Crisis Mentality

Among the many elements shared by the institutions of the crisis triangle is the crisis-driven nature of foreign policy, headline news, and humanitarian action. Despite institutional needs, pressures, and cultures that tend to focus minds and resources on the present, all three institutions would benefit from looking further ahead. However great the need for each institution to review individually its performance, doing so together also has special value. The fact that public opinion waxes hot and cold on humanitarian crises suggests that the process of institutional reflection will need to be sustained by the actors on their own.

8.5.4. Cooperation on Media Matters

The most likely common ground for building cooperation within the institutional triangle is more accurate and urgent coverage of headline news, with greater audience impact. Documentary and commentary news will continue to provide the most fertile are of cooperation to address the root causes of complex emergencies - but, however welcome by policymakers and humanitarian organisations, greater depth, continuity, and sophistication will be sought by the media only when their public demands it. Whatever the state of public awareness, the news media provide one of the few common platforms on which complex emergencies can be debated and undergo arbitration among the various external actors. Governments and humanitarian organisations may resist having a full-fledged public debate on their policies and practices on "opinion pages" or talk shows.

In democratic societies, however, that is a major device for articulating interests and hammering out consensus. All institutions can benefit from the town meeting function of the media. The dangers of the perennial short-term focus of governments and aid groups on emergency responses and the absence of strategy to deal with the new world disorder can be highlighted while the media exercises a public service role in the process. Although each of the three institutions working in civil wars can benefit from greater cooperation, increased contact among them is unlikely to replace the current mistrust and distance with altogether harmonious or synergistic interaction - nor should it. Each set of institutions has and will continue to have its own agendas, constituencies, procedures, mandates, and accountabilities. The media will not cease to play a watchdog role simply because government policymakers and aid officials seek to forge more effective working relationships with them.

At the same time, more collegial working relationships with the media will improve both policy and action. Benefits of a humanitarian nature should accrue from the media's potential to move public opinion and power elites at critical moments in the policy process. Better coverage, better policy, and better action would result from the three institutions tempering their normal crisis perspectives and higher levels of professionalism and greater collaboration between the three should be urged.

8.6. Media Relations

Good media relations are rooted in trust. Journalists need immediate and unimpeded access to sources of information and must be able to rely on the veracity of their sources. Like reputation, credibility is a fragile object. Once credibility is lost, it is not easily regained. Those who try to manipulate the media, for example, by exaggerating refugee numbers and suffering, overstating agency accomplishments, or suppressing important facts, may gain positive coverage in the short-term but will lose out in the long-term. An individual's credibility can be enhanced or undermined by their agency's credibility, and vice versa thus, the importance of clear and consistent agency procedures.

8.6.1. Honestness

Respond honestly and accurately. Tension can arise in trying to accommodate the media when a person is not in a position to supply credible information, or s/he need more time to prepare it. Inadvertent provisional, inaccurate or misleading information can undermine credibility.

8.6.2. Be Prompt, Available and Helpful

Provide reporters with prompt answers to their queries. Whenever feasible, facilitate the media's access to useful and accurate information. At a practical level, this may mean helping them gain privileged access to conflict zones and interviews with major players in the emergency or conflict.

8.6.3. Provide Factual and Concrete Information

Provide accurate facts and figures about the emergency and activities. Journalists want factual information on the number of refugees/returnees, methods of transport, dates of displacement and return, country and place of origin, names of other agencies in the operation, major humanitarian assistance needs, sources of funding, appeal figures, as well as human interest stories for domestic audiences.

8.6.4. Understand Media Priorities and Interests

Effective media relations depend on understanding the priorities, interests and needs of the various news media sources.

8.6.5. Be Open and Transparent

Journalists also want to know about the problems journalists face and what they are doing to overcome these difficulties.

8.6.6. Nurture Constructive Media Contacts

Humanitarian agencies should spend considerable resources nurturing constructive working relationships with the news media. Nurtured over time, these contacts give greater confidence to media professionals, encouraging them to proceed with important stories for which full collaboration is time-consuming or impossible. Personal contacts are equally important with gatekeepers in the system, such as editors and owners.

8.6.6.1. Diversify media contacts

By virtue of their personal motivations, some journalists may be easier to engage in the humanitarian sphere than others. There should be no presumption, however, that the news media are involved for any reason other than to produce objective reporting. Since headline news necessarily remains an ever-changing forum, agencies should make greater use of documentary and commentary news to stimulate more thoughtful policy debate about complex emergencies in which humanitarian organisations have a strong interest.

There is fierce competition for headline news; agencies should not overlook opinion page columnists, feature writers, and documentary filmmakers who often have the luxury to consider subjects beyond the main news. A good concerted media strategy, whether of an individual organisation or a coalition of aid groups, will allow for differentiated approaches depending on the objectives being advanced.

8.6.6.2. Press conference

Agencies hold press conferences to publicly announce significant and newsworthy initiatives, changes in policy or official statements regarding controversial issues to a variety of news media outlets. The basic rule for press conferences is to have something significant to announce and somebody significant to announce it. Nothing else works. If overused, or inappropriately used, people will stop attending them and your credibility with the news media will be damaged. Little irks reporters more than a badly timed, ill-considered press conference of limited news value.

8.6.6.3. Press releases

A press release is a brief written statement, under a page long, which announces a significant agency policy, initiative or real-life story. Press releases should be written in a newspaper format and convey the basic who, what, when, where, how and why of the story. A carefully crafted, well written and well-timed press release gives reporters a ready-made story, or something they can quickly edit, cut or rewrite, according to their needs and time constraints.

8.6.6.4. Editorials

Editorial writers differ from news reporters in that their writing reflects more idealism, advocacy and personal opinion. Every day they must find an issue or topic to announce, denounce, expose, praise, analyse and comment on. Their purpose is to further the debate, influence public opinion and shape public policy on issues of concern to them. Good editorial writers, however, will want to learn all sides of an issue prior to establishing their own opinion.

8.6.6.5. News documentaries

Documentary news, which enjoys a longer shelf life than headline news, may offer more detailed background and analysis of an issue, demonstrating the investigative or analytical skills of a particular news outlet or reporter. This kind of coverage is typically found in specialist broadcast features and on inside pages of newspapers and journals. Some newspapers have little space for documentary news and, in their allocation of what they have, give preference to local or national over international topics. Documentary news can stimulate more thoughtful policy debate about complex emergencies, and provide a more complete image of a developing country and the challenges it faces.

References

Frost, Gary and Silverman, Randy, "Disaster recovery in the artefact fields – Mississippi after Hurricane Katrina", *International Preservation News,* 2005.

Hooghiemstra, R., "Corporate communication and impression management - new perspectives why companies engage in corporate social reporting", *Journal of Business Ethics*, 27(1/2): 55-69, 2000.

Miller, D.S., "A construction of competing disaster narratives: media coverage of the distribution of risk following a technological disaster", [Ph.D. Thesis] Mississippi State University, 1997.

Taboroff, June, "Natural disasters and urban cultural heritage: a reassessment", in: Kreimer, Alcira, Arnold, Margaret and Carlin, Anne (eds.) *Building safer cities: the future of disaster risk*, Washington D.C.: World Bank, 2003.

CHAPTER 9

Rehabilitation of Victims

9.1. Introduction

Rehabilitation refers to the actions taken in the aftermath of a disaster to enable basic services to resume functioning, assist victims' self-help efforts to repair physical damage and community facilities, revive economic activities and provide support for the psychological and social well being of the survivors. It focuses on enabling the affected population to resume more-or-less normal (pre-disaster) patterns of life. It may be considered as a transitional phase between immediate relief and more major, long-term development.

Reconstruction refers to the full restoration of all services, and local infrastructure, replacement of damaged physical structures, the revitalisation of economy and the restoration of social and cultural life. Reconstruction must be fully integrated into long-term development plans, taking into account future disaster risks and possibilities to reduce such risks by incorporating appropriate measures. Damaged structures and services may not necessarily be restored in their previous form or location. It may include the replacement of any temporary arrangements established as part of emergency response or rehabilitation.

To amplify the two definitions, following a damaging hurricane the rehabilitation of the power lines would aim to restore the system as rapidly as possible so that the essential services would continue to function. Whereas, reconstruction of the power lines should aim to rebuild the rehabilitated system to a higher or safer standard than before so that the future risks to the power lines from a similar damaging event would be reduced. Sometimes, the term recovery is also used to embrace both activities. It should be remembered that rehabilitation and reconstruction actions do not always safeguard full recovery. It may take longer to return to 'normality' or, in some situations, recovery may never be possible. It is, therefore, not possible to suggest a 'model' time frame for rehabilitation, reconstruction or recovery as distinctive periods. The length of time required for rehabilitation and reconstruction depends on a large number of factors, including pre-disaster trends, the extent of damage, level of preparedness, availability of resources, administrative and legislative powers to act rapidly, and political stability and will to implement plans.

Furthermore, different sectors may vary in the time required to rehabilitate or reconstruct. For example, infrastructure requiring high levels of investment and sophisticated technology may take a very long time to fully rebuild to a higher standard. Similarly, economic setbacks due to a disaster can take time to recover from, and in some situations, a return to pre-disaster levels of production may never be possible. This will particularly apply where the disaster interrupted a key economic activity, thus allowing competitors the opportunity to intercept the market and hold onto it when recovery has been attained.

The social and psychological recovery of the affected population are often assumed to be a community function and neglected in most post-disaster programmes. Although this may be true for some societies, disasters can render some groups such as the elderly without an immediate family, orphans, single parents with young children more vulnerable due to a lack of adequate support. In the aftermath of a disaster family support systems can break down due to life losses, dislocation and migration of some members in search of work, food etc.

These groups would need special social support to survive the impact of disaster. Similar to social disruption, the psychological trauma of losing relatives and friends, the shock of the disaster event can take much longer to heal than physical recovery. It is, therefore, essential that social welfare and psychological support programmes are considered immediately after a disaster as an integral part of recovery programmes. This support should be provided not only for the affected public but also for the aid workers and the authorities operating in the disaster area as they can also become psychologically distressed from the event and working in difficult conditions.

9.2. Scope of Rehabilitation

Each disaster results in a different type of damage. However, on the basis of past events the sectors that will be at risk to a particular disaster can be predicted with some accuracy. For example, earthquakes often result in high physical damage to infrastructure and buildings and high winds can destroy both buildings and utilities above ground such as power lines. Floods, on the other hand, can be damaging for agricultural land and fisheries in rural areas, which would not be affected by earthquake impact. Planning for rehabilitation and reconstruction should therefore relate to the specific damage that results from a disaster and prioritise inputs to assist the rapid recovery of the affected population. For example, after a rural flood, replacing the lost livestock or seeds for the next planting season might be a higher priority for rural agriculturists than the rebuilding of their homes. Following the 1992 floods in Pakistan much of the government grants allocated for damaged houses were used by the communities to buy animals, fodder and seeds.

While physical damage may vary from one type of disaster to another, all major disasters have a psychological impact on the affected population as well as disrupting economic and social life of the survivors. In addition, all major disasters have significant political consequences, which have sometimes resulted in the weakening of authorities, or the strengthening of weak ones as a result of their positive handling of the recovery process. Therefore, rehabilitation and reconstruction programmes should not only be seen as a way of replacing what is tangible but must be planned to strengthen what is not immediately visible, that is, the administrative, social and economic systems as well as the psychological well being of the people involved.

9.2.1. Scale and Location

The scale and location of the disaster damage are critical in understanding the type of inputs required for rehabilitation and reconstruction. The ratio of what is lost or damaged to what has survived influences the nature of recovery. A localised event which affects a relatively limited area in a country, for example an earthquake in a city, needs to be treated in a different manner than a situation where the whole country might be affected by a devastating event for example a hurricane which hits a small island. In a large country it is likely that there will be adequate surviving material and human resources, and facilities to rehabilitate the situation whereas for a small country the same event may result in the loss of most facilities and resources that are needed for rehabilitation and reconstruction. A thorough evaluation of the local and national resources is essential before determining what is needed to be provided from outside.

Location of a disaster is critical in understanding the sectors affected and the rehabilitation and reconstruction implications of the event. The sectors that are vulnerable to the same type of disaster vary from one area to another. While psychological needs may not vary greatly in relation to location for the same type of event, social, economic and physical damage can display a different pattern in urban and rural areas. Rural areas are likely to have less infrastructure and concentration of administrative, commercial and industrial facilities but more agriculture and livestock than urban centers. The priorities for recovery and reconstruction inputs clearly need to reflect this difference. For example, replacing the livestock, agricultural tools and seeds after a rural flood will often be seen as vital for rapid recovery by the affected population. Whereas in an urban flood, rehabilitation of the damaged infrastructure will be essential for renewed functioning of the economy.

Special problems that may arise in some urban disasters, especially in developing countries, lie in the concentration of administrative, political, commercial and cultural facilities in the cities, often in the capital. Heavy losses in a major city, therefore, can have a negative impact on the capacity for rapid decision-making and long-term resources, which are much needed for rapid recovery. consequently, assessing the capacities of public and private institutions following a disaster and rebuilding or supporting them where they are inadequate should be considered before moving into other aspects of reconstruction planning.

Location of the disaster also determines the possibility of secondary effects. For example, heavy rainfall and earthquakes in areas with steep slopes can trigger landslides. Damage to dams, bridges and industrial plants by natural events may lead to future disasters. Reconstruction and relocation decisions need to incorporate such secondary risks that may arise from the possible location of the event. These potential threats need to be evaluated especially in planning for physical rehabilitation and reconstruction projects. Failure to do so may result in reducing one risk at the cost of creating another one. Another critical issue in relation to the location of a disaster is the limited attention that might be given to some affected areas vis-a-vis others which attract disproportionate support. This may be due to a number of factors. Sometimes selective media coverage shapes the nature of subsequent support. It is the big city in relation to small villages, or, the center of the event as opposed to the peripheries that receive the most attention even at times when there are only a few survivors. The Armero volcanic mudflow in Colombia is a classical example of this situation where the relocated town was built much larger than was needed for the very few survivors to benefit from the reconstruction. More often, however, it is the areas where ethnically, politically, economically or socially marginalised communities live that are overlooked. As these groups may not always be in a position to effectively articulate their needs, rehabilitation and reconstruction programmes can easily neglect them as beneficiaries.

Rehabilitation and especially reconstruction often refer to the repair and rebuilding of the physical damage. Authorities and donors focus on the provision of housing, clinics, schools and eventually rebuilding of the infrastructure. As already emphasised in this module, the non-physical damage such as the psychological impact of the event, economic losses, social and cultural disruption to community life can be often overlooked. The concentration on physical reconstruction is essential for a return to normality and is demanded by society. It is also an easily quantifiable and visible achievement for the authorities and donors. Social, psychological, cultural and even economic recovery is less tangible for government, agency or donor investment and is seen in most cases at the responsibility of the community.

A comprehensive rehabilitation and reconstruction plan should take into consideration both physical and non-physical needs of the communities. Failing to address reconstruction in its complexity can have adverse consequences-firstly it may result in large investment on buildings without the necessary inputs to help the victims to become psychologically fit, socially coherent and economically self-sustained. Secondly, it is important to recognise the links between physical and socio/psychological recovery. For example, the process of disaster victims being active in their own physical rebuilding can have an important economical and therapeutic value. Thus double dividends may result from their active involvement in physical rebuilding. Rehabilitation and reconstruction programs that encourage the affected population to act together in their own interest can also have psychological benefit as well as reducing dependency on external inputs. The sectors that need rehabilitation and reconstruction inputs relate to the disaster type and the elements that are at risk.

Balancing needs with resources is critical at stages of post-disaster activities. While the relief period may attract large national and international inputs, rehabilitation and reconstruction may not benefit from such high levels of attention. Prioritisation of investment becomes critical where monetary resources are limited and sectoral needs are too many to meet.

In disasters of considerable magnitude, not only various sectors but also a large number of counties, municipalities or settlements are often competing for the same funds and for the attention of the same authorities and expertise. Strong community or administrative leadership is critical at this stage in marshaling national and international support. Local administrative preparedness plans and general capacity, together with technical mechanisms that are in place before the disaster, usually contribute significantly to expeditious recovery. Although some dependence on external resources is to be expected after a large-scale disaster, excessive dependence can cause loss of local control and delays in recovery. Small communities that have sustained heavy damage are most likely to become dependent on external inputs of this kind. In such circumstances resources should be channeled to enhance local capacities to cope with the effects of disasters and to maximise community self-reliance.

Efforts should not duplicate or provide what can be locally available or undertaken. Consultation with the local agencies and the affected population is essential in this process as the Donor's or the authorities perception of what is critical and essential may differ significantly from local perceptions. In this respect, the role of external assistance should be to identify strengths and bottlenecks in order to mobilise the necessary resources that are not available and cannot be generated at the local or national level. The bottlenecks for speedy recovery vary greatly from country to country, area to area.

Recovery from major disaster events necessitate large quantities of material and human resources and good organisational/ institutional capacity. Although there may be various national and international organisations to support the local population in recovering from the impact of the event much of the responsibility for rehabilitation and reconstruction will fall on the government of the country concerned. Besides, effective recovery response very much depends on the authorities capacity to plan and coordinate the efforts of the various groups involved in this process.

Facilitating all these actions requires political commitment of the government for the benefit of the disaster stricken areas. However, channeling of funds, allocating resources of all kinds, providing services and opportunities for recovery often happens in a political context. Electoral pressures and local power structures may become instrumental in shaping the nature of reconstruction. While most governments in the immediate aftermath of a disaster declare their intentions of making up for all losses, with the progress of time, they can easily lose the initial momentum. As media attention drops, the public loses faith in receiving support and the authorities shift their focus on other issues.

Recovery will be delayed. In some situations such as civil conflict there may not be real commitment to begin with. The speed and effectiveness of recovery, therefore, is as much a political issue as it is a matter of resources. In this respect, the nature of rehabilitation and reconstruction planning will be greatly shaped by the level of political commitment and its sustainability throughout the process.

9.3. Stages of Reconstruction

Although rehabilitation and reconstruction are distinctive activities, they should not be seen in isolation from other pre- and post-disaster actions. Reconstruction after a disaster provides many mitigation and development opportunities that may not be possible in 'normal' conditions. If properly utilised, these opportunities can, in return, improve the effectiveness of recovery from possible future disasters. Similarly, integration of rehabilitation planning into local and national preparedness plans contributes to better recovery.

9.3.1. Mitigation into Reconstruction

Ideally, reconstruction should aim to build to a better standard than existed before. Any actions to improve the pre-disaster conditions can help to reduce disaster risk and mitigate the damage of future events. There are several structural and non-structural mitigation measures that are discussed in the module Disaster Mitigation.

9.3.2. Reconstruction and Development

Post-disaster reconstruction can influence development programmes both positively and negatively. Similarly, the pre-disaster level of development in a country will have a bearing upon the success of recovery and reconstruction. Past examples prove that in areas of low pre-disaster development, recovery will be slow or, sometimes, can never be achieved. Delays in reconstruction will also decrease public and private investments, divert resources away from development activities to sustaining rehabilitation over an extended period of time. Productive capital takes a particularly long time to replace in the case of agriculture and stock breeding, which may result in migration from the disaster stricken area.

Reduced industrial output, on the other hand, can lead to wage losses, unemployment and disruption of dependent economic activities. While loans and subsidies can act as emergency economic measures, reconstruction programmes need to be planned with close consideration of the likely developmental status of the affected area. Since disasters often hit the least developed areas and the most disadvantaged groups hardest, rehabilitation and reconstruction programmes should also aim to change the vulnerable conditions for the high risk population through development programmes. These conditions can be much more deep rooted than they seem on the surface when revealed by disaster, such as lack of access to information, limited economic means to maintain safety, environmental degradation, lack of social networks or limited political power. A wide range of examples of developmental inputs in post-disaster programs to address some of the root causes of vulnerability are in the Disasters and Development module.

9.4. Reconstruction and Preparedness Plans

Conventional preparedness plans often include stockpiling of food, shelter, medicine, tools etc. for emergency and rehabilitation needs. Increasingly, however, the advantages of incorporating reconstruction needs into preparedness plans is becoming obvious.

9.4.1. Emergency Relief into Rehabilitation

Although emergency relief is a distinctive stage of post-disaster activities, many of the actions and decisions of this period can influence later stages. Extended external relief assistance can undermine local and national coping capacity and create dependency.

Large scale damaging events, often with pressures from the media, result in large amounts of international relief which leaves limited resources for the long-term recovery and rehabilitation.

Continuity of support by agencies and donor governments beyond relief needs to be considered at early stages of allocating funds and other resources in a more balanced way. Articulation of rehabilitation and reconstruction needs into relief appeals and ways of integrating relief and long-term assistance also need to be explored.

While assessment of damage, needs and resources need to be specific and prioritised for the task at hand, i.e. relief, often rehabilitation and reconstruction decisions are based on these early data. This is partly due to the cost and time it takes to collect data and to meet the public demand to act rapidly. Ideally, it is necessary to monitor the changing needs as the situation develops. However, this may not be the case after most disasters. This common pattern needs to be recognised. Therefore, the drawbacks of early be taken into account in the planning of rehabilitation and reconstruction. During the early stages of disaster response it is important to plan the co-ordination of data collection, multi-disciplinary assessment teams, and data generation for later phases. This will improve the quality and effectiveness of early information for rapid rehabilitation and reconstruction decisions.

However, it should be remembered that as conditions change, decisions need to be modified in light of updated information. For example, after a major earthquake the number of homeless is often calculated in relation to damaged or destroyed buildings. However, due to the fear of after shocks, the public may refuse to go back to their surviving homes, which will increase the need for shelter provision beyond the initial assessment. While it is important to recognise patterns from early diagnostic indicators for rapid response, decisions to effect long-term actions should not be taken in the haste of relief operations. Decisions such as relocation or provision of temporary shelters require careful examination of their long-term implications and consultation with the communities. There are many examples of temporary shelter provision as a response to an early identified need, which eventually became permanent at great cost and often in wrong locations. Similarly, medical programmes or food distribution should not be prolonged without monitoring of the changes at the local level.

9.4.2. Guiding Principles

9.4.2.1. Political support

Support will be at its highest in the aftermath of the disaster and will gradually decrease in time. Pre-election time often increases the political will to act swiftly. Effective leadership and organisational capacity at the local level can put pressure on the authorities for the sustainability of political support. Better media coverage beyond the initial relief phase can also help to put pressure on the authorities. Ways of keeping the interest of the media to follow up progress with recovery needs should be sought. Professional bodies and community organisations can also be considered among the pressure groups to maintain political interest.

Most national and international funding will be available during the relief and sometimes rehabilitation periods. As reconstruction needs increase, often available funds are decreased. At this stage local income generation, revolving funds, and private sector support and other funding possibilities are essential. The above assumptions can be represented in graphic form which indicate that paradoxically, political and media support needed to maintain funding for reconstruction is apt to decline just as implementation gets under way, just when it is most needed.

9.4.2.2. Rehabilitation and reconstruction processes

The complex nature of the recovery phase, the large number of actors involved from the press, donors, various authorities to the different interest groups at community level often result in conflict of perceptions, concerns and values not to mention difference of opinions among the technical community. This will run through the whole process from the needs assessment to the final stage of reconstruction. These conflicts can delay the recovery process considerably, and if not resolved by active collaboration of all parties, may result in unsatisfactory programmes.

9.4.2.3. Tasks

Depending on the scale of damage and the country's level of development, there may be lack of skilled human resources and administrative capacity to facilitate the necessary actions. The import of external expertise can help fill the gap in the short-term but may not be maintained in the long-term. Training and education will improve the situation but pre-disaster investment in human development will be the key. Maximising the local capacities in self-reliance rather than depending on external support and aiming for programmes that can increase local involvement will also reduce the need for 'expert' inputs in some aspects of recovery.

Reconstruction can provide extensive work opportunities with the potential for profits for building contractors. Unless authorities maintain effective quality control and enforcement, there is a real risk that the seeds of the next disaster can be sown at this time. Delays in reconstruction decisions, land allocation, micro zonation, new codes, provision of materials and expertise etc., can also result in the public taking its own actions to repair or rebuild without proper guidance and control by the authorities. In such situations it may still be better to make some sacrifices and act from available information and emergency codes rather than delay all actions for more thorough scientific studies. Likewise, mitigation measures that are acceptable and affordable by the vulnerable groups may have a chance of reducing future risks more than sophisticated measures that cannot be implemented or maintained by the affected population.

Government officials and politicians regularly make this assumption. To initiate building codes or land-use planning controls is one thing, to enforce them over time is another. It will be particularly difficult to ensure the obedience of poor families who cannot afford the extra expense of the code requirements or who have no access to safe land. One option will be to link codes and controls with some form of subsidy or incentives, and training for the public as well as inspection to ensure that the resources are available to ensure that compliance occurs. Nevertheless, it will still be optimistic to assume that marginal settlements and most rural areas will benefit from codes and controls without comprehensive planning that incorporates their wide spectrum of needs to achieve safety.

9.4.2.4. Pre-disaster planning

Officials must recognise that before effective implementation of any reconstruction it will be imperative to look at the administrative system, planning procedures, codes of practice, quality control systems, land ownership, local power structures, general standards of living etc. The problem that is often faced is that authorities find themselves undertaking a double reconstruction process; they are reconstructing the failures of the system in reducing disaster risk and vulnerabilities, as well as post-disaster reconstruction.

9.5. Dilemmas and Alternatives

There are many dilemmas that decision makers face in planning for rehabilitation and reconstruction. Each set of actors involved in the process, such as the central government, local authorities, various sectors, a large variety of professionals, donors, NGOs and different segments of the community, is likely to have different priorities and perceptions and subsequently would like to act according to their own preferences. There are always alternatives, and before a decision is made on a course of action their shortcomings, advantages and long-term implications need to be evaluated. Failure to recognise these conflicts and alternatives can create resistance by one group or the other and can ultimately hinder the progress of decision-making. Some of the likely dilemmas and alternatives in rehabilitation and reconstruction planning cover the following issues.

Consequential losses from damage to agriculture or business premises may require evaluation by economists; accurate definition of building damage requires inspection by structural engineers. Detailed damage assessment can also help to determine the causes of damage, and the sources of risks and vulnerability. As this level of information becomes available, planning tasks can be more precisely defined. The dilemmas concerning detailed technical surveys usually relate to the time it takes to complete the surveys, and the appropriateness of this information for the user.

9.5.1. Repairs Vs Rebuilding

Restoration of services and lifelines through repairs after a major disaster is a high priority as rebuilding can be delayed considerably an requires high levels of investment, and sometimes technology. Quick repair of buildings, especially domestic buildings, on the other hand, is usually discouraged by the authorities who prefer detailed technical inspection, improved codes and identifying the safety of land. The dilemma is the trade off between rapid repairs of rebuilding to higher standards, which may take longer to plan. Quick repairs, however, can alleviate some of the need for temporary housing and public facilities. In fact, domestic repairs are often carried out by individuals if decisions are delayed.

9.5.2. Safety Standards Vs Rapid Reconstruction

Evaluation of the causes of losses, risks and vulnerabilities after a major disaster can be complicated, expensive and time consuming. Yet they are essential for improving the safety standards against future damaging events. Lack of safe land to build on and setting new safety standards can equally delay reconstruction decisions. Without security of land and tenure it will also be wrong to expect people to invest in safety. Pre-disaster planning for post-disaster reconstruction must address land use issues in advance. Existing general information can be useful in identifying where reconstruction can begin without further studies. Phasing in decisions and prioritising areas for different safety standards can help to start reconstruction.

9.5.3. Special Organisation Vs Existing Organisation

A wide range of organisational structures for rehabilitation and reconstruction have been used after major disasters. Existing organisations often have the staff and resources but may not have the procedures to act rapidly. Emergency powers granted to existing institutions can expedite decisions concerning rapid rehabilitation. Reconstruction on the other hand can take a long time and requires a clear structure, resources and authority to oversee the work. Sometimes one agency, department or ministry can be designated with support from others. However, more often some new organisation is needed to plan and manage rebuilding. The dilemma is that the existing organisations will have staff and other resources, which a new organisation has to create. But the new organisation will have the special authority and power to handle reconstruction more independently and rapidly.

A further problem with the creation of a new organisation is that pre-disaster collaboration and coordination of various groups and institutions for better rehabilitation and reconstruction preparedness will be limited. Ultimately, the choice will depend on the specific conditions in each country and in each situation. The critical issues in any organisational structure will be the co-ordination of all relevant agencies and institutions and the mobilisation of resources. A high level Rehabilitation and Reconstruction Commission can be effective. It should also be remembered that in some special situations such as conflict-induced disasters or where loss of life among the officials is high there may be a need for rebuilding the capacities of necessary institutions.

9.5.4. Public Vs Private Investment

Public funds are usually available for rehabilitation and rebuilding of public facilities, but they can also extend into supporting rehabilitation of the economy and domestic losses such as buildings or assets. However, public investment alone is never sufficient to bring about full recovery nor does it necessarily help to develop an effective strategy for rebuilding. Private investment is more likely to happen in areas, which are economically strong and are not perceived as high risk. International and public inputs into economic recovery can create confidence for private investors to invest in rebuilding. Such funds can also be useful as loans to pay for reconstruction to be recovered eventually. Even in centrally controlled economies and with paternalistic governments, total reliance on public funds may delay recovery considerably. In fact, such situations may raise expectation, create dependency and bring private investment to a complete halt. Furthermore, heavy government or international assistance may delay or reduce the willingness to take self-help actions.

9.5.5. Physical Reconstruction Vs Economic Rehabilitation

Governments face a dilemma following any disaster that causes extensive damage to both the local economy and to the physical environment. Both demands require immediate attention and the deployment of extensive resources. In a rich country the two sectors are likely to be fully addressed in parallel, but in a poor country the overwhelming financial and administrative burden may be such that choices have to be made about which should have priority attention and at what stage in the reconstruction process. There is a growing awareness by many governments and international funders of the need to regenerate damaged economy - whether agricultural or industrial - as rapidly as possible. The logic is that if the damaged economy can get back on its feet rapidly then this can be one of the 'motors' to drive physical rebuilding.

9.5.6. Local Resources Vs Imported Resources

Effective reconstruction requires skill, labor and materials. It also requires them in a vastly greater quantity than normal demand. Therefore, officials tend to look in all directions for the support they need. This is a natural and necessary response, but a dilemma remains whether to select local versus imported people or products. The advantage of local resources is the obvious need to strengthen the local economy, which may have been significantly damaged or disrupted.

However, local resources may be inadequate for the task, therefore external support may be essential to close the gap between needs and resources. It is also clear that some aspects of reconstruction require expert skills and knowledge which has to come from other parts of a country or from international sources.

9.6. Guiding Principles

Planning and management of rehabilitation and reconstruction are highly complex processes that cover a sequence of actions from data collection to assessment of needs, planning, implementation and evaluation. Recovery actions embrace numerous sectors of society and involve actions by individuals, communities, governments and international bodies. Although similarities exist between one recovery situation and another, each case has unique characteristics, diverse patterns of damage, different needs, varied constraints and levels of resources. Therefore, given such variables, only very general principles can be established.

It is not a platitude to state that recovery after disaster poses a challenge. It can easily become a series of lost opportunities: minimal advances in safety, protracted years, even decades of unfinished projects and an economy that has failed to reach pre-disaster levels of productivity. But, with careful planning, conscientious management and the full commitment of a society it can be regarded as a unique opportunity to bring many benefits which can lead to an improved natural and built environment.

References

James F. Miskel, *Disaster Response and Homeland Security: What Works, What Doesn't*, Praeger Publishers Inc, US, 2006.

Prabhas Chandra Sinha, *Disaster Relief: Rehabilitation and Emergency Humanitarian Assistance*, SBS Publishers, 2006.

Stephen Arno & Steven Allison-Burnell, *Flames in Our Forest: Disaster or Renewal?*, Island Press, 2002.

Bibliography

Albala-Bertrand, J.M., *Political economy of large natural disasters: with special reference to developing countries,* Oxford: Clarendon Press, 1993.

Alexander, D., *Principles of Emergency planning and Management*, Harpended: Terra publishing, 2002,

.........., "The Study of Natural Disasters 1977-1997: Some Reflections on a Changing Field of Knowledge", *Disasters* 21 (4): 284-304, 1997.

.........., *Natural Disasters*, London: Routledge, 2002.

Allen, E., "Political Responses to Flood Disaster: The Case of Rio De Janeiro", 1988, In A. Varley (Ed.) *Disasters, Development and the Environment.* London: Belhaven, 1994.

Armenian, H. K., A. K. Melkonian, and A. P. Hovanesian, "Long-Term Mortality and Morbidity Related to Degree of Damage Following the Earthquake in Armenia", *American Journal of Epidemiology,* 1998.

Baker, Earl J., "Hurricane Evacuation Behavior", *International Journal of Mass Emergencies and Disasters,* 1991.

.........., "Hurricane Evacuation in the United States", Pp. 306-319 in Storms Volume I. London: Routledge, 2000.

.........., "Predicting Response to Hurricane Warnings: A Reanalysis of Data fromFour Studies", *Mass Emergencies,* 1979.

.........., "Public Response to Hurricane Probability Forecasts", *Professional Geographer*, 1995.

Baker, Jay, "Warning and Evacuation in Hurricanes Elena and Kate", *Tallahassee,* FL: Department of Geography, Florida State University, 1987.

Balluz, L., L. Schieve, T. Holmes, S. Kiezak, J. Malilay, "Predictors for People's Response to a Tornado Warning: Arkansas, 1 March 1997", *Disasters*, 2000.

Berke, P., Kartez, J. and Wenger, D., "Recovery after Disaster: Achieving Sustainable Development, Mitigation and Equity", *Disasters,* 1993.

Bernstein, R. S., P. J. Baxter, and A. S. Buist, "Introduction to the Epidemiological Aspects of Explosive Volcanism", *American Journal of Public Health,* 1986.

Bhatta, Braja Bandhu, *The natural calamities in Orissa in the 19th century*, New Delhi: Commonwealth Publishers, 1997.

Bohem, Hilda. Disaster Prevention and Disaster Preparedness . Berkeley: University of California, 1978.

Buist, A. S., and R. S. Bernstein, "Health Effects of Volcanoes: An Approach to Evaluating the Health Effects of an Environmental Hazard", *American Journal of Public Health* 76 (Suppl.):1-2, 1986.

Bulgawicz, Susan L. and Charles E. Nolan. Disaster Prevention and Recovery: A Planned Approach, Prairie Village: ARMA International, 1988.

Burton, I., Kates, R.W. and White, G.F., *The Environment as Hazard, Second Edition,* New York/London: Guilford Press, 1993.

Cannon, T., "Vulnerability Analysis and the Explanation of 'Natural' Disasters", In Varley, A. (Ed.) *Disasters, Development and the Environment:* 13-30, London: Belhaven Press, 1994.

Carter, N., *Disaster Management, a disaster Manager's Handbook,* Asian Development Bank, Manilla, 1991.

Chang, S. E., and C. Chamberlin, "Assessing the Role of Lifeline Systems in Community Disaster Resilience", *In Research Progress and Accomplishments 2003-2004, Multidisciplinary Center for Earthquake Engineering Research*, Buffalo, NY: 87-94, 2004.

Coburn, A.W., Spence, R.J.S. and Pomonis, A., "Vulnerability and Risk Assessment", *UNDP Disaster Management Training Program,* 1991.

Comfort, Louise K., ed. *Managing Disaster: Strategies and Policy Perspectives*, Durham: Duke University Press, 1988.

Fitzpatrick, Colleen and Dennis S. Mileti, "Perception and Response to Aftershock Warnings During the Emergency Period", Pp. 75-83 in *The Loma Prieta Earthquake: Studies of Short-Term Impacts,* Monograph No. 50, edited by R. Bolin. Boulder, CO: Natural Hazards Research and Applications Information Center, Institute of Behavioral Science, University of Colorado, 1990.

Freeman, P.K., L. Martin, J. Linnerooth-Bayer, R. Mechler, K. Warner and G. Pflug, "Disaster Risk Management: Financial Strategies for Natural Disaster Reconstruction", *Regional Policy Dialogue on National Systems for Comprehensive Disaster Management*, Washington DC, Inter-American, Development Bank, 2002.

Frost, Gary and Silverman, Randy, "Disaster recovery in the artefact fields – Mississippi after Hurricane Katrina", *International Preservation News,* 2005.

Genovese, Robert, Trish Taylor and Edward White, *Disaster Preparedness Manual*, Buffalo, N.Y. : W.S. Hein, 1989.

Gupta, H.K. (ed.), *Latur earthquake*, Bangalore : Geological Society of India, 1994.

Haddow, George D. and Jane A. Bullock, *Introduction to Emergency Management*, Amsterdam: Butterworth-Heinemann, 2003.

Hooghiemstra, R., "Corporate communication and impression management - new perspectives why companies engage in corporate social reporting", *Journal of Business Ethics*, 27(1/2): 55-69, 2000.

Howard, M. J., J. C. Brillman, and F. M. Burkle, "Infectious Disease Emergencies in Disasters", *Emergency Medicine Clinics in North America* 14 (2): 413-28, 1996.

James F. Miskel, *Disaster Response and Homeland Security: What Works, What Doesn't*, Praeger Publishers Inc, US, 2006.

Kelly, P.M. and W.N. Adger, "Theory and Practice in Assessing Vulnerability to Climate Change and Facilitating Adaptation. Climatic Change, 2000.

Lindell, Michael K., Ronald W. Perry, and Marjorie R. Greene, "Race and Disaster Warning Response." Seattle, WA: Battelle Human Affairs Research Centers, 1980.

Mack, Raymond W. and George W. Baker, "The Occasion Instant: The Structure of Social Responses to Repeated Air Raid Warnings", Washington, D.C.: National Research Council, National Academy of Sciences, 1961.

Malilay, J., M. G. Real, A. Ramirez Vanegas, E. Noji, and T. Sinks, "Public Health Surveillance after a Volcanic Eruption: Lessons from Cerro Negro, Nicaragua, 1992", *Bulletin of the Pan American Health Organization,* 1996.

Mathieson, David, "Hurricane Preparedness: Establishing Workable Policies for Dealing with Storm Threats", *Technology and Conservation,* Summer 1983.

Mileti, Dennis S. and Paul W. O'Brien, "Warnings During Disaster: Normalizing Communicated Risk", *Social Problems,* 1992.

Miller, D.S., "A construction of competing disaster narratives: media coverage of the distribution of risk following a technological disaster", [Ph.D. Thesis] Mississippi State University, 1997.

Morgan, O., "Infectious Disease Risks from Dead Bodies Following Natural Disasters", *Revista Panamericana de Salud Publica,* 2004.

Parker, D. (Ed.), *Floods,* 2 vols., London: Routledge, 2000.

Prabhas Chandra Sinha, *Disaster Relief: Rehabilitation and Emergency Humanitarian Assistance*, SBS Publishers, 2006.

Quarantelli, E.L., *What is a disaster - Perspectives on the question*, New York: Routledge, 1998.

Seaman, J., Leivesley, S. and Hogg, C., *Epidemiology of Natural Disasters,* Basel: Karger, 1984.

Sharma, Vinod K. (ed.), *Disaster management*, New Delhi: National Centre for Disaster Management, Indian Institute of Public Administration, 2001.

Smit, B., I. Burton, R.J.T. Klein and R. Street, "The Science of Adaptation: A Framework for Assessment", *Mitigation and Adaptation Strategies for Global Change*, 1999.

Stephen Arno & Steven Allison-Burnell, *Flames in Our Forest: Disaster or Renewal?*, Island Press, 2002.

Suryanarayana, M., "Marine fisherfolk of north-east coastal Andhra Pradesh", Calcutta: Anthropological Survey of India, Govt. of India, 1977.

Taboroff, June, "Natural disasters and urban cultural heritage: a reassessment", in: Kreimer, Alcira, Arnold, Margaret and Carlin, Anne (eds.) *Building safer cities: the future of disaster risk*, Washington D.C.: World Bank, 2003.

Wisner, B., P. Blaikie, T. Cannon, and I. Davis, *At Risk - Natural hazards, people's vulnerability and disasters*, Wiltshire: Routledge, 2004.